Oxford Skills World

Reading

with Writing

1

Sarah Jane Lewis-Mantzaris

OXFORD

UNIVERSITY PRESS

OXFORD
UNIVERSITY PRESS

198 Madison Avenue
New York, NY 10016 USA

Great Clarendon Street, Oxford, OX2 6DP, United Kingdom

Oxford University Press is a department of the University of Oxford.
It furthers the University's objective of excellence in research, scholarship,
and education by publishing worldwide. Oxford is a registered trade
mark of Oxford University Press in the UK and in certain other countries

ISBN: 978 0 19 411346 5 Student Book with Workbook

Printed in China

This book is printed on paper from certified and well-managed sources

ACKNOWLEDGMENTS

*Oxford University Press would like to thank all of the teachers whose opinions helped to
inform this series, and in particular, the following reviewers:* Soo Ah Chung, Hwarang
Elementary School; Marta Juanet, Betania-patmos; Sedef Toksoz Kaygin,
Denizli Pamukkale Unv Egitim Vakfi okullari (PEV Koleji); Jeehee Moon,
T.T.R.; Jacob Rod, WILS Language School; Yuechun Wang, Phoenix City
International School

Cover illustration and main character illustrations by: Shane McGowan/The
Organisation

Back cover photograph: Oxford University Press building/David Fisher

Student Book

Illustrations by: Robin Boyer/Illustration Online pp.15, 25, 29, 43, 55, 64, 85;
Mattia Cerato/MB Artists pp.36, 54, 78; Pascale Constantin pp.12, 37, 88;
Monique Dong/Bright Group p.51; Lalena Fisher pp.9, 11, 18, 38, 39, 44, 47,
53, 60, 74; Sarah Jennings/Bright Group p.41; John Kurtz pp.69, 71, 82, 83,
84, 86; Anthony Lewis/MB Artists pp.8, 26, 50, 68; Steffane McClary/Maggie
Byer-Sprinzeles pp.13, 14, 40, 57, 58; Julissa Mora pp.16, 67, 79, 80, 81; Laura
Watson/Illustration Online p.27

*The Publishers would like to thank the following for their kind permission to reproduce
photographs and other copyright material:* 123rf: pp.9 (waste basket/Micael
Nussbaumer), 10 (pedal bin/destinacigdem), (empty bookcases/shutswis),
22 (two guinea pigs/Zdenek Precechtel), 24 (budgie/Busakorn Pongparnit),
27 (horse wearing saddle/elen1), (frog/Aliaksei Hintau), 28 (horse eating
hay/Goce Risteski), (turtle on grass/Kathy Clark), 42 (heart-shaped balloon/
Vitalina Rybakova), (traingular kite/Pavel Losevsky), 52 (multi-coloured jump
rope/Zoltan Ladislau Kiraly), (toy robot/Charles Taylor), 55 (orange juice/
Sergei Vinogradov), (pizza/Boris Ryzhkov), 56 (smoothie with straws/Inga
Nielsen), 65 (sunny beach/Igor Goncharenko), (hot boy drinking/Anurak
Ponapatimet), 69 (girl with umbrella/pat138241), 72 (child with umbrella/
Robbie Schubert), 79 (baby sister/malija), (brother/Wavebreak Media Ltd);
Alamy: pp.62–63 (children in wind/Brian Scantlebury /Alamy Stock Photo);
Getty: pp.cover (boy and plane/Peter Beavis), 6–7 (school children/Westend61),
9 (desk/Jeffrey Coolidge), 48–49 (father and son/Brand X Pictures), 65 (Inuit
boy/Johner Images), 76–77 (Chinese latern festival/Andre Vogelaere); OUP:
pp.9 (red chair/Shutterstock), 13 (yellow pencil/Dennis Kitchen Studio, Inc.),
(marker pens/Dennis Kitchen Studio, Inc.), 22 (backpack/Shutterstock),
23 (dog/Shutterstock), (cat/Shutterstock), (parrot/Shutterstock), (hamster/
Shutterstock), 28 (rabbit on grass/Shutterstock), (garden frog/Shutterstock),
32 (tree frog/Shutterstock), 51 (jump rope/Shutterstock), (toy robot/
Shutterstock), 52 (rag doll/Shutterstock), 55 (chocolate cake/Shutterstock),
56 (apple and apple juice/Shutterstock), 70 (lightning storm/Shutterstock);
Shutterstock: pp.9 (bookcase/donatas1205), 10 (child's desk/Kletr), (blue chair/
binbeter), 13 (pencil case/Gulgun Ozaktas), (crayon/Yellow Cat),
19 (pencil, reused on pp.47, 61, 75, 89 /almaje), 20–21 (elephant swimming/

Willyam Bradberry), 22 (cichlid fish/Torsten Dietrich), (giraffes/Andrzej
Kubik), 23 (boy with dog/unguryanu), 24 (dog in park/Chendongshan),
(hamster in sawdust/stock_shot), (cat in garden/LiAndStudio), 27 (turtle/
Tim Zurowski), (rabbit/kwhw), 30 (guide dog with person/goodluz), (hamster
in wheel/AtiwatPhotography), 34–35 (artwork/camp camera), 42 (box kite/
KPG_Payless), (blue balloon/Michael Dechev), 51 (rag doll/Pao Laroid), (orange
yo-yo/navee sangvitoon), 52 (purple yo-yo/Olga Galkina), 55 (smoothie/Patricia
Hofmeester), 56 (chocolate cake slice/Amawasri Pakdara), (pizza slice/Evgeniy
Ovchinnikov), 65 (condensing breath/pavla), (children in snow/Vladimir
Konstantinov), 66 (child by lake/Maria Evseyeva), (snowy village/Vadim
Nefedoff), (village in sunshine/Vadim Petrakov), (woman by coastline/Vadim
Petrakov), 69 (cloudy sky/Imagentle), (girl windy day/S Curtis), 69 (storm
forming/Kento35), 70 (clouds over city/Phillip Maguire), (woman walking with
umbrella/Bogoshipda), (woman in wind/nelen), 79 (father/Fotoluminate LLC),
(mother/Blend Images)

Workbook

Illustrations by: Robin Boyer/Illustration Online pp.98, 114; Mattia Cerato/MB
Artists p.100 (Ex C3a); Pascale Constantin pp.99 105; Monique Dong p.103;
Lalena Fisher pp.91, 100 (Ex C1, C2, C3b, C4), 101; John Kurtz pp.112, 113;
Anthony Lewis/MB Artists p.97; Steffane McClary/Maggie Byers-Sprinzeles
pp.93, 94, 108 (Ex C3b); Julissa Mora pp.108 (Ex C4a), 109

*The Publishers would like to thank the following for their kind permission to
reproduce photographs and other copyright material:* 123rf: pp.92 (waste basket/
Micael Nussbaumer), 96 (horse wearing saddle/elen1), 98 (turtle on grass/
Kathy Clark), (horse eating hay/Goce Risteski), 102 (triangular kite/Pavel
Losevsky), (heart shaped balloon/Vitalina Rybakova), 104 (green toy robot/
Charles Taylor), 106 (smoothie with straws/Inga Nielsen), 108 (cold child/
Jasmin Merdan), (hot boy drinking/Anurak Ponapatimet), (sunny beach/
Igor Goncharenko); OUP: pp.92 (wooden door/Shutterstock), (red chair/
Shutterstock), (wooden table/123rf), (backpack/Shutterstock), 96 (parrot/
Shutterstock), (cat /Shutterstock), (hamster/Shutterstock), (dog/Shutterstock),
98 (garden frog/Shutterstock), (rabbit on grass/Shutterstock), 104 (yellow toy
robot/Shutterstock), (brown rag doll/Shutterstock), (jump rope/Shutterstock),
106 (apple and apple juice/Shutterstock), 107 (woman viewing Rome/
Shutterstock), (view of Perth/Shutterstock), 108 (snowman/Shutterstock), 110
(lightning storm/Shutterstock), 111 (boy/
Shutterstock); Shutterstock: pp.92 (child's desk/Kletr), (blue chair/binbeter),
(bookcase/donatas1205), 95 (hamster in wheel/AtiwatPhotography), 96 (cat in
garden/LiAndStudio), (dog in park/Chendongshan), (rabbit/kwhw), 102 (blue
balloon/Michael Dechev), (box kite/KPG_Payless), 104 (colourful rag doll/Pao
Laroid), (pencil case/Gulgun Ozaktas), (purple yo-yo/Olga Galkina),
106 (chocolate cake slice/Amawasri Pakdara), (pizza slice/Evgeniy
Ovchinnikov), 108 (condensing breath/pavla), (children in snow/Vladimir
Konstantinov), 110 (cloudy sky/Imagentle), (woman in wind/nelen)

Table of Contents

Hi! I'm Olly.

Hi, I'm Molly!

Introduction

Welcome to Oxford Skills World

Oxford Skills World: Reading with Writing is a flexible paired skills course that takes students on a journey toward independent learning, providing them with strategies and support to reach their goals.

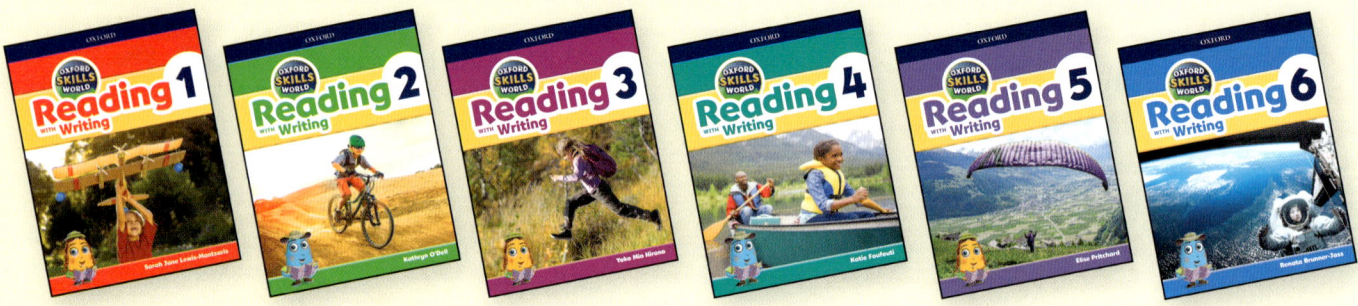

For Students

- Student Book / Workbook
- Student's website with downloadable audio and extra resources
  www.oup.com/elt/oxfordskillsworld

For Teachers

- Downloadable Teacher's Pack with instructional support, assessment, professional development videos, projects, and writing resources
- Classroom Presentation Tool
- Teacher's website with downloadable audio and extra resources
  www.oup.com/elt/teacher/oxfordskillsworld

Be the Leader on Your Skills Adventure!

Hi! We're Olly and Molly, your skills adventure guides. We help you reach your goals by introducing new reading and writing strategies, asking helpful questions, and giving friendly reminders. Most importantly, we cheer you on every step of the way! Let's go!

Quick Guide

Inside Each Topic

Topic Opener

Theme-based topics provide high-interest content relevant to students' lives.

My Goals introduces students to the objectives of each unit in the topic.*

Fun characters, Olly and Molly, encourage 21st century skills like critical thinking, collaboration, and communication.

Students answer questions to activate prior knowledge and think critically.

Get Ready to Read • Read

Reading Goals are strategies students can apply to any text.

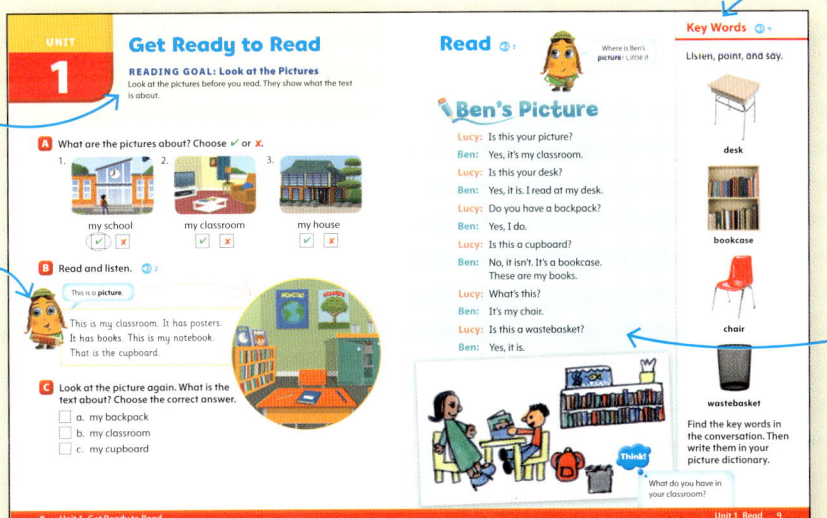

Students learn new vocabulary for each text and complete the picture dictionary at the back of the book.

Olly and Molly guide students as they learn and apply new reading strategies.

Students apply strategies to high-interest fiction and nonfiction texts, think critically about what they read, and make connections to their own lives.

*Each topic contains two thematically related units.

Quick Guide

Understand

Students increase their comprehension of the text by applying reading strategies to what they have read.

Students complete activities to strengthen their understanding of the unit's vocabulary.

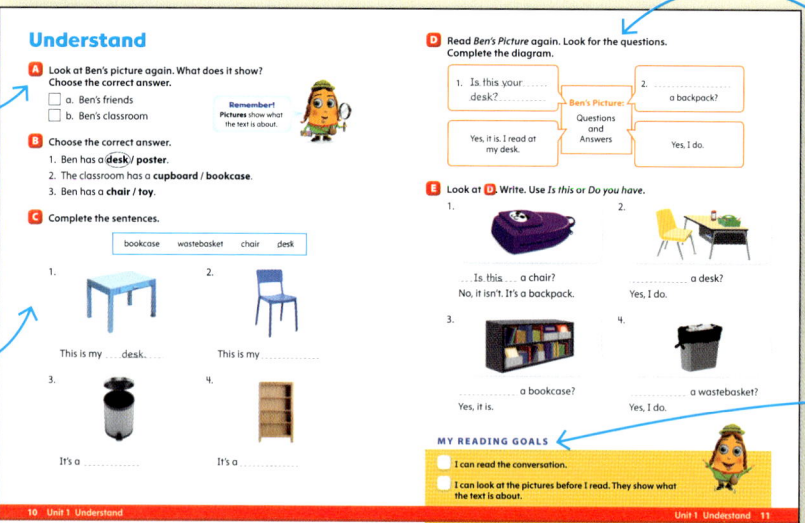

Students demonstrate comprehension of the unit's text, vocabulary, and grammar.

At the end of each unit, students assess the progress they have made toward achieving their goals.

Reading Check

With helpful reminders from Olly and Molly, students apply the **Reading Goals** from both units to a new text.

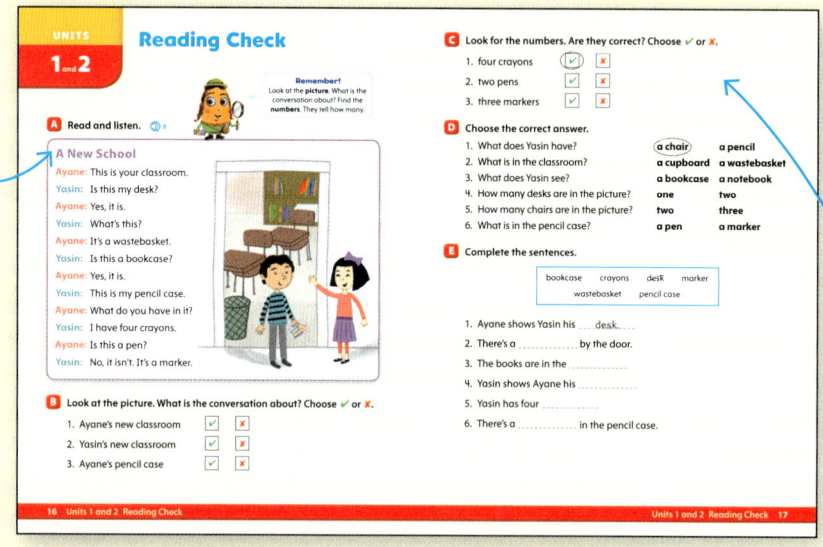

Students complete activities to boost comprehension and vocabulary application.

Get Ready to Write • Write

Writing Goals prepare students to write in different genres.

Writing Tips provide guidance on grammar, punctuation, and mechanics and help students write fluently and accurately.

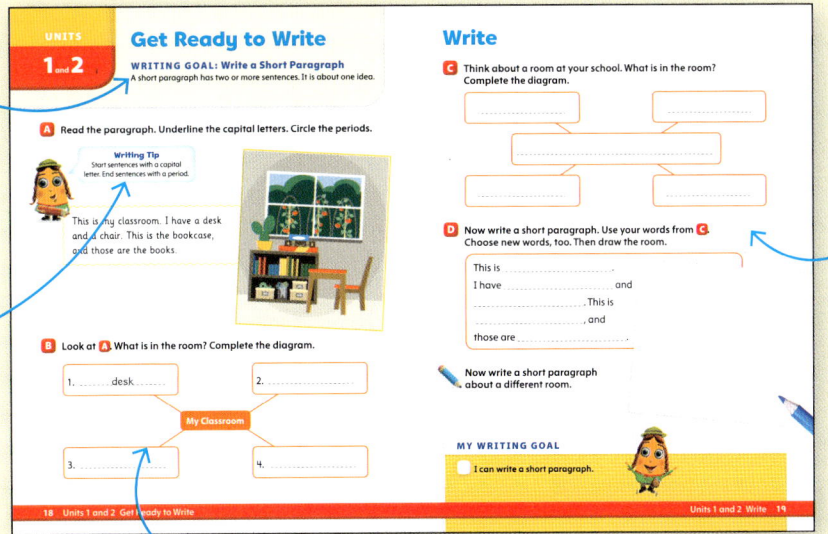

Scaffolded writing passages help students accomplish their writing goals.

Students use graphic organizers to comprehend model writing texts and to organize their thoughts for their own writing.

Workbook

Workbook pages at the end of the book provide more opportunities for students to apply their **Reading Goals** and boost comprehension.

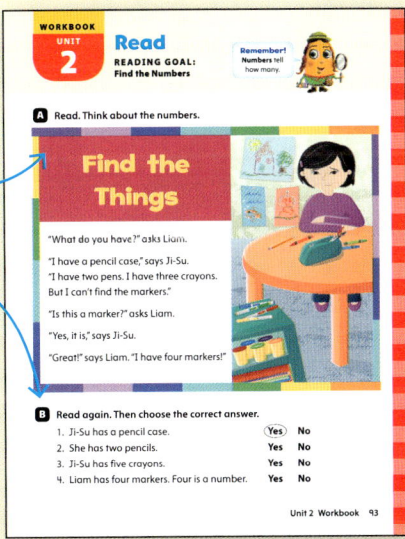

Additional activities provide extra opportunities for vocabulary comprehension and usage.

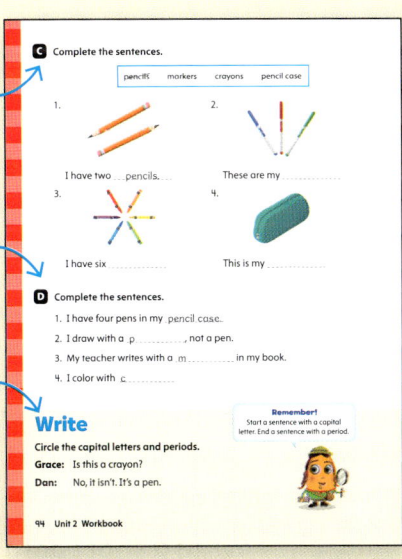

Students apply the topic's **Writing Tip** to ensure proper usage in their own writing.

In Your School

MY GOALS

UNIT 1
- Read the conversation *Ben's Picture*
- Look at the pictures

UNIT 2
- Read the story *The Pencil Case*
- Find the numbers

WRITE
- Write a short paragraph

A Look at the picture. What do you see?

1. How many children are there?
2. Where are the children?

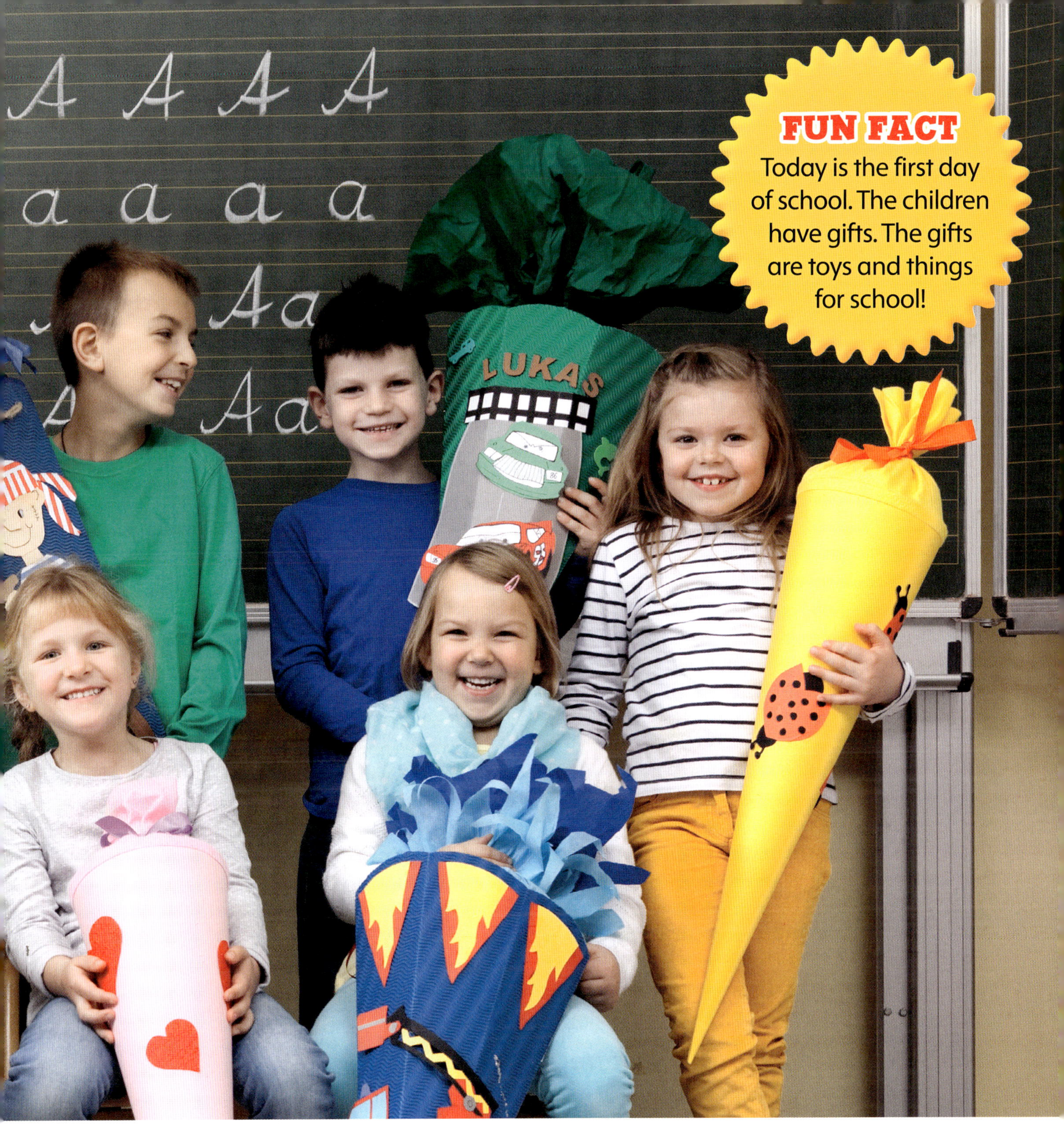

B Read the Fun Fact. Then answer the questions.

1. What do the children have?

2. What things do you have for school?

Think, Pair, Share

What do you do in school?

Get Ready to Read

READING GOAL: Look at the Pictures
Look at the pictures before you read. They show what the text is about.

A What are the pictures about? Choose ✔ or ✗.

1.

my school

2.

my classroom

3.

my house

B Read and listen. 🔊 2

This is a **picture**.

This is my classroom. It has posters.
It has books. This is my notebook.
That is the cupboard.

C Look at the picture again. What is the text about? Choose the correct answer.

☐ a. my backpack
☐ b. my classroom
☐ c. my cupboard

Read  🔊 3

Where is Ben's **picture**? Circle it.

Ben's Picture

Lucy: Is this your picture?

Ben: Yes, it's my classroom.

Lucy: Is this your desk?

Ben: Yes, it is. I read at my desk.

Lucy: Do you have a backpack?

Ben: Yes, I do.

Lucy: Is this a cupboard?

Ben: No, it isn't. It's a bookcase.
These are my books.

Lucy: What's this?

Ben: It's my chair.

Lucy: Is this a wastebasket?

Ben: Yes, it is.

Think!

What do you have in
your classroom?

Key Words 🔊 4

Listen, point, and say.

desk

bookcase

chair

wastebasket

Find the key words in
the conversation. Then
write them in your
picture dictionary.

Understand

A Look at Ben's picture again. What does it show?
Choose the correct answer.

☐ a. Ben's friends

☐ b. Ben's classroom

Remember!
Pictures show what the text is about.

B Choose the correct answer.

1. Ben has a **desk** / **poster**.

2. The classroom has a **cupboard** / **bookcase**.

3. Ben has a **chair** / **toy**.

C Complete the sentences.

| bookcase | wastebasket | chair | desk |

1.

This is my ____desk.____

2.

This is my _____

3.

It's a _____

4.

It's a _____

D Read *Ben's Picture* again. Look for the questions. Complete the diagram.

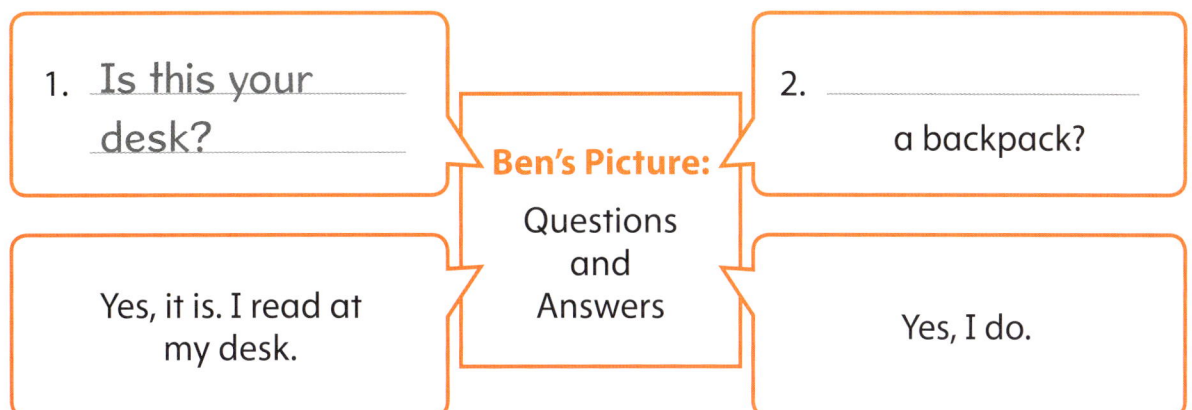

1. Is this your desk?

Yes, it is. I read at my desk.

Ben's Picture: Questions and Answers

2. _____ a backpack?

Yes, I do.

E Look at **D**. Write. Use *Is this* or *Do you have*.

1.

    Is this   a chair?
No, it isn't. It's a backpack.

2.

_____ a desk?
Yes, I do.

3.

_____ a bookcase?
Yes, it is.

4.

_____ a wastebasket?
Yes, I do.

MY READING GOALS

☐ I can read the conversation.

☐ I can look at the pictures before I read. They show what the text is about.

Get Ready to Read

READING GOAL: Find the Numbers
We can write numbers: *1, 2, 3*. We can spell numbers: *one, two, three*. Find the numbers when you read. They tell how many.

A **What do you see? Circle the numbers.**

B **Read and listen.** 🔊 5

These are **numbers**.

"This is my backpack," says Hugo.
"It's big!" says Alice. "What do you have in it?"
"I have three books," says Hugo. "I also have five pens!"

C **Read B again. Choose ✔ or ✗.**

	✔	✗
1. Hugo has two backpacks.		⊗
2. He has three books.	✔	
3. He has three pens.	✔	

Read 🔊 6

Where are the **numbers**? Underline them.

The Pencil Case

"I can't find my pencil case!" says Mi-Jin.

"Is this your pencil case?" asks Alan.

"No, that's Lily's pencil case. She has two pens. I have two pencils."

"Do you have crayons?" asks Alan.

"Yes," says Mi-Jin. "I have six crayons."

"You have three markers, too!" says Alan. "I see your pencil case. It's on the bookcase!"

Think!

Do you have a pencil case? What do you have in it?

Listen, point, and say.

pencil case

pencil

crayon

marker

Find the key words in the story. Then write them in your picture dictionary.

Understand

A Read *The Pencil Case* again. Look at the numbers. Choose **Yes** or **No**.

1. Mi-Jin has four pencils.   **Yes**   (**No**)

2. She has two crayons.   **Yes**   **No**

3. She has three markers.   **Yes**   **No**

> **Remember!**
> **Numbers** tell how many.

B Choose the correct answer.

1. What does Alan find?
   - ☐ a. a backpack
   - ☑ b. a pencil case

2. How many pens does Lily have?
   - ☐ a. two
   - ☐ b. three

3. Does Mi-Jin have a pen?
   - ☐ a. Yes, she does.
   - ☐ b. No, she doesn't.

C Complete the sentences with key words. Then match.

1. Lily has a <u>pencil case.</u>

2. Mi-Jin has two _____

3. Mi-Jin has six _____

4. She has three _____

a. _____

b. _____

c. _____

d. _____1_____

D Read *The Pencil Case* again. Complete the diagram.

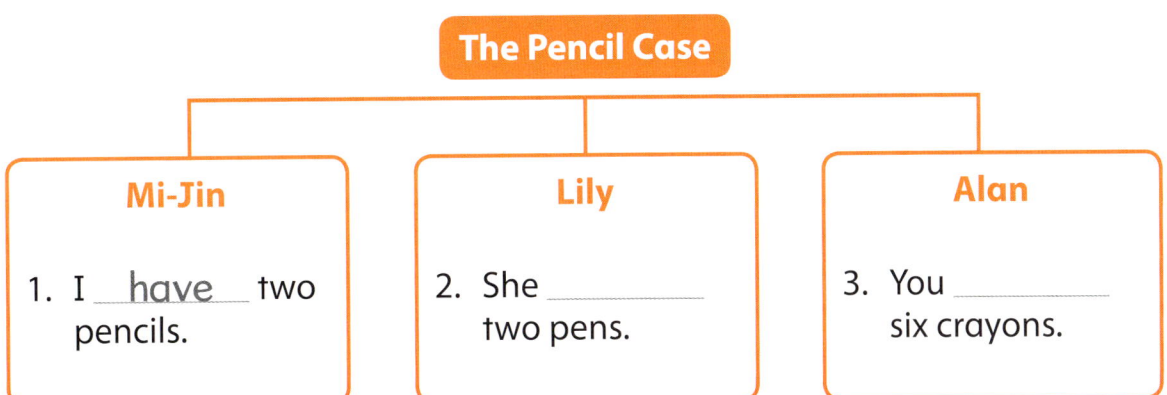

The Pencil Case

Mi-Jin

1. I __have__ two pencils.

Lily

2. She _____ two pens.

Alan

3. You _____ six crayons.

E Look at **D**. Write. Use *have* or *has*.

1.

I __have__ three pencils.

2.

She _____ two pencil cases.

3.

You _____ four crayons.

4.

He _____ five markers.

MY READING GOALS

☐ I can read the story.

☐ I can find the numbers when I read. They tell how many.

Reading Check

A Read and listen. 8

A New School

Ayane: This is your classroom.

Yasin: Is this my desk?

Ayane: Yes, it is.

Yasin: What's this?

Ayane: It's a wastebasket.

Yasin: Is this a bookcase?

Ayane: Yes, it is.

Yasin: This is my pencil case.

Ayane: What do you have in it?

Yasin: I have four crayons.

Ayane: Is this a pen?

Yasin: No, it isn't. It's a marker.

B Look at the picture. What is the conversation about? Choose ✔ or ✘.

1. Ayane's new classroom

2. Yasin's new classroom

3. Ayane's pencil case

C Look for the numbers. Are they correct? Choose ✔ or ✘.

1. four crayons ✔(circled) ✘
2. two pens ✔ ✘
3. three markers ✔ ✘

D Choose the correct answer.

1. What does Yasin have?   a chair (circled)   a pencil
2. What is in the classroom?   a cupboard   a wastebasket
3. What does Yasin see?   a bookcase   a notebook
4. How many desks are in the picture?   one   two
5. How many chairs are in the picture?   two   three
6. What is in the pencil case?   a pen   a marker

E Complete the sentences.

> bookcase   crayons   ~~desk~~   marker
>
> wastebasket   pencil case

1. Ayane shows Yasin his ___desk.___
2. There's a _____ by the door.
3. The books are in the _____
4. Yasin shows Ayane his _____
5. Yasin has four _____
6. There's a _____ in the pencil case.

Get Ready to Write

WRITING GOAL: Write a Short Paragraph

A short paragraph has two or more sentences. It is about one idea.

A Read the paragraph. Underline the capital letters. Circle the periods.

Writing Tip
Start sentences with a capital letter. End sentences with a period.

This is my classroom. I have a desk and a chair. This is the bookcase, and those are the books.

B Look at **A**. What is in the room? Complete the diagram.

1. _____desk_____

2. _____

My Classroom

3. _____

4. _____

Write

C Think about a room at your school. What is in the room? Complete the diagram.

```
┌─────────────────────┐              ┌─────────────────────┐
│ _____ │              │ _____ │
└─────────────────────┘              └─────────────────────┘
            ┌─────────────────────────────────┐
            │ _____ │
            └─────────────────────────────────┘
┌─────────────────────┐              ┌─────────────────────┐
│ _____ │              │ _____ │
└─────────────────────┘              └─────────────────────┘
```

D Now write a short paragraph. Use your words from **C**. Choose new words, too. Then draw the room.

This is _____.

I have _____ and

_____. This is

_____, and

those are _____.

Now write a short paragraph about a different room.

MY WRITING GOAL

☐ I can write a short paragraph.

Animals

MY GOALS

UNIT 3

- Read the text *Four Fun Pets*
- Read the title

UNIT 4

- Read the story *The Right Pet*
- Read the captions

WRITE

- Write an informational paragraph

A Look at the picture. What do you see?

1. Where is the elephant?
2. How many legs does the elephant have?

FUN FACT

Elephants like water. They use their legs and feet. They can go 48 kilometers!

B Read the Fun Fact. Then answer the questions.

1. What do elephants like?

2. What other animals like water?

Think, Pair, Share
What animals do you like?

Get Ready to Read

READING GOAL: Read the Title

A title is the text's name. It tells what the text is about. Look at the title before you read. Guess what the text is about.

A Look at the pictures. Choose the correct title.

1.

☐ a. My Notebook
☑ b. My Backpack

2.

☐ a. My Pets
☐ b. My Toys

3.

head
eye
tail
mouth

☐ a. Parts of a Fish
☐ b. Parts of the Face

B Read and listen. 🔊 9

This is the **title**.

Big Giraffes

Giraffes are big. A baby giraffe is 1.8 meters tall. Giraffes have big legs and feet. They have good eyes and ears.

C Read the title again. What is the text about? Choose the correct answer.

☐ a. Giraffes like trees.

☐ b. Giraffes are fast.

☐ c. Giraffes are big.

Read  🔊 10

Where is the **title**? Underline it.

Four Fun Pets

Dogs 🐾
Dogs can run and jump. Some dogs are big.

Cats 🐾
Cats are clean. They sleep a lot. They can see well at night.

Birds ✗
Lots of people have pet birds. Some birds can talk.

Hamsters 🐾
Hamsters have little ears and big eyes. They can't see well.

Think!

What pet do you like? What can it do?

Key Words 🔊 11

Listen, point, and say.

dog

cat

bird

hamster

Find the key words in the text. Then write them in your picture dictionary.

Understand

A Read the title again. What is *Four Fun Pets* about?
Choose the correct answer.

Remember!
The **title** tells what
the text is about.

☐ a. big animals

☐ b. pet animals

B Choose the correct answer.

1. Dogs (can) / can't jump.

2. Cats **sleep** / **eat** a lot.

3. Hamsters have **little** / **big** ears.

C Complete the sentences.

~~dog~~	cat	hamster	bird

1.

This ___dog___ is big.

2.

This _____ can talk.

3.

A _____ has big eyes.

4.

A _____ can see well
at night.

D Complete the diagram.

What can animals do?				
	Dog	**Cat**	**Bird**	**Hamster**
1. can see well at night				
2. can run and jump	✔			
3. can fly				
4. can't see well				

E Look at **D**. Write. Use *can* or *can't*.

1.

Dogs __can__ run and jump.

2.

Birds _____ fly.

3.

Cats _____ see well at night.

4.

Hamsters _____ see well.

MY READING GOALS

☐ I can read the text.

☐ I can read the title. I can guess what the text is about.

Get Ready to Read

READING GOAL: Read the Captions

Sometimes there are words under a picture. These words are a caption. A caption gives information about the picture. Look at captions when you read to learn about a story.

A Look at the captions. Put the pictures in order: *1, 2, 3*.

The bird says, "Thank you!"

The bird eats.

1

The children go to the zoo.

B Read and listen. 12

This is a **caption**.

Do you like dogs? This dog can ride a skateboard! He rides his skateboard at the park.

Bill on his skateboard

C Read **B** again. What does the caption tell you about the story? Choose ✔ or ✗.

1. Bill has a dog.

2. The dog's name is Bill.

3. Dogs are good pets.

Read 🔊 13

Where is the **caption**? Underline it.

The Right Pet

Sam wants a pet. He likes horses, but his mom says they're too big. "A frog is little," she says. "I don't like frogs," says Sam. "Do you like turtles?" she asks. "They can't play," says Sam.

She shows Sam a picture. "I like rabbits," he says. "Let's go!" says his mom.

Sam's new pet

Think!

What can rabbits do?

Key Words 🔊 14

Listen, point, and say.

horse

frog

turtle

rabbit

Find the key words in the story. Then write them in your picture dictionary.

Understand

A Read *The Right Pet* again. What does the caption tell you about the story? Choose **Yes** or **No**.

1. Sam gets a new pet.   **Yes**   **No**
2. Sam likes rabbits.   **Yes**   **No**
3. Sam has two pets.   **Yes**   **No**

Remember!
A **caption** helps you understand a story.

B Choose the correct answer.

1. What animals are little?
   ☐ a. horses   ✔ b. frogs
2. What animals doesn't Sam like?
   ☐ a. horses   ☐ b. frogs
3. What can't turtles do?
   ☐ a. play   ☐ b. walk

C Complete the sentences with key words. Then match.

1. A ___horse___ is big.

2. A _____ can't play.

3. A _____ has big ears.

4. A _____ is little. It jumps a lot.

a.    b.    c.    d.

_____   ___1___   _____   _____

D Read *The Right Pet* again. What animals does Sam like? What animals doesn't Sam like? Complete the diagram.

	I like	I don't like
1. horses	✔	
2. frogs		
3. turtles		
4. rabbits		

E Look at **D**. Write. Use *like* or *don't like*.

1.

I ____like____ horses.

2.

I _____ spiders.

3.

I _____ tigers.

4.

I _____ snakes.

MY READING GOALS

☐ I can read the story.　　☐ I can read the captions. They tell about the pictures and the story.

Reading Check

Remember!
Read the **title**. What is the text about? Read the **captions**. What do they tell you?

A Read and listen. 15

A Good Pet for You

Dogs are fun. They can play. Cats, birds, and rabbits can play, too. Turtles and frogs can't play.

Some birds can talk. You can ride horses.

Turtles and frogs are little. Rabbits and hamsters are little, too. Horses are big.

What pet do you like?

Dogs can help.

Hamsters can play.

B Look at the title. What is the text about? Choose ✔ or ✗.

1. fun pets

2. the right pet ✗

3. happy pets

C Look at the captions. What do they tell you about the animals? Choose ✔ or ✘.

1. They can help and play. ✔ ✘

2. They can run. ✔ ✘

3. They're clean. ✔ ✘

D Choose the correct answer.

1. A _____ can help. ☐ a. cat   ✔ b. dog

2. A _____ can't play. ☐ a. dog   ☐ b. turtle

3. Some _____ can talk. ☐ a. birds   ☐ b. frogs

4. Rabbits and hamsters are _____ ☐ a. big.   ☐ b. little.

5. A _____ is big. ☐ a. horse   ☐ b. turtle

E Unscramble and match.

1. t c a

_____cat_____

2. d g o

_____

3. b i d r

_____

4. b r a b i t

_____

5. m e r t s a h

_____

6. h e r s o

_____

a. This animal can fly.

b. This animal can see well at night.

c. This animal has little ears and big eyes.

d. You can ride it.

e. This animal can help.

f. This animal can play.

Get Ready to Write

WRITING GOAL: Write an Informational Paragraph
An informational paragraph is true. It has real information about a topic. It can be about a person, a place, or a thing.

A Read the informational paragraph. Underline the picture and caption.

> **Writing Tip**
> Use a picture and a caption to give more information.

Red-Eyed Tree Frog

The red-eyed tree frog lives in trees. It has big toes. It eats at night.

The red-eyed tree frog is little.

B Look at **A**. Find the information. Complete the diagram.

lives	has
1. _____ in trees _____	2. _____

Red-Eyed Tree Frog

does at night

3. _____

Write

C Think about your pet or a different animal. Complete the diagram.

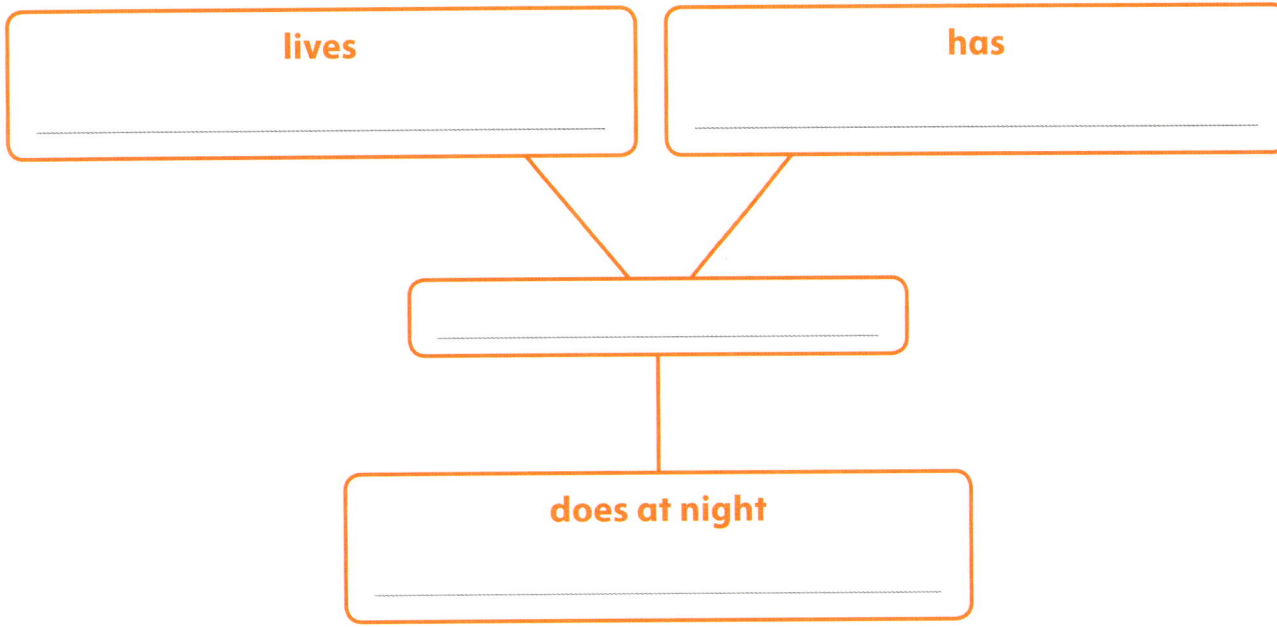

lives

_____

has

_____

_____

does at night

_____

D Now write an informational paragraph. Use your words from **C**. Choose new words, too. Then draw the animal. Write a caption.

_____ lives

_____ .

It has _____ .

It _____ at night.

Now write an informational paragraph about a new animal.

Caption:

_____

☐ I can write an informational paragraph.

TOPIC 3
ART

Colors and Shapes

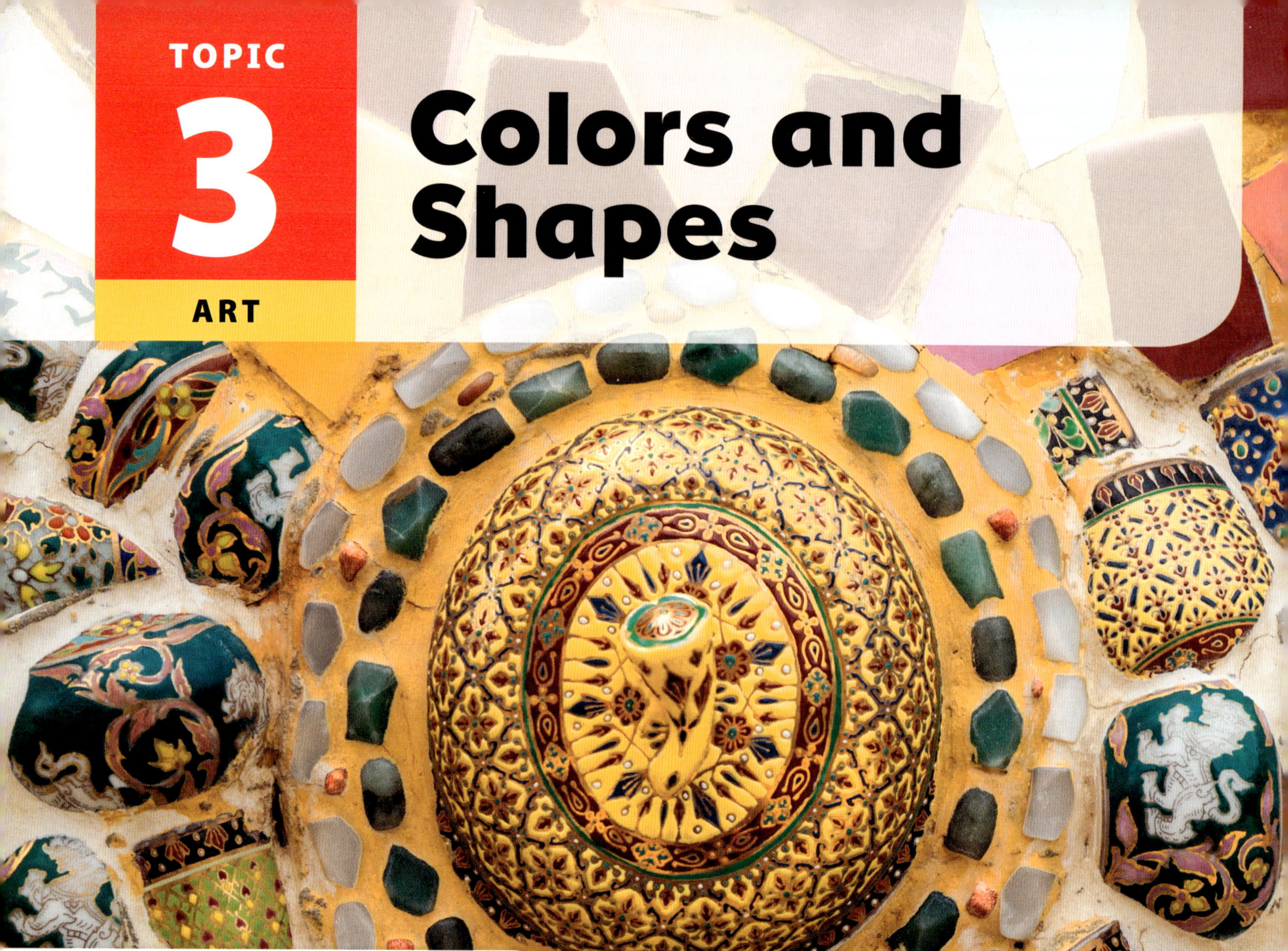

MY GOALS

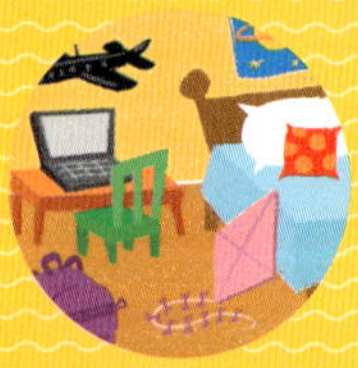

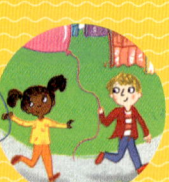

UNIT 5

- Read the text *Max's Room*
- Find the color words

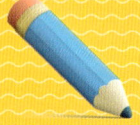

UNIT 6

- Read the story *Shapes at the Park*
- Find the shape words

WRITE

- Write a description

A Look at the picture. What do you see?

1. What colors do you see?
2. Do you like what you see? Why or why not?

FUN FACT

This is a mosaic. People can make mosaics with many things. Some mosaics are very old. They can be little or very big.

B Read the Fun Fact. Then answer the questions.

1. Can mosaics be little?
2. Where can you see art?

Think, Pair, Share
What art do you make?

Get Ready to Read

READING GOAL: Find the Color Words
Words like *red* and *green* are color words. Find the color words
when you read. They tell what color things are.

A **Look at the pictures. Choose the correct answer.**

1.

It's a **green /**
blue jacket.

2.

It's a **green /**
yellow backpack.

3.

It's a **red /**
blue poster.

B **Read and listen.** 🔊 16

These are **color words**.

Pictures

I draw and color pictures. This is my
balloon. It's red. This is my bike.
It's green. This is my teddy bear.
It's brown.

C **Read B again. What color is the balloon?**
Choose the correct answer.

☐ a. red

☐ b. green

☐ c. brown

Read 17

Where are the **color words**? Underline them.

← → ↻ www.studentsandart.osw

Max's Room by Cara

Max: This is my room.

Cara: I like it! What color is this room?

Max: It's orange.

Cara: Is this a black plane?

Max: Yes, it is.

Cara: What color is this backpack?

Max: It's purple.

Cara: Is this a pink kite?

Max: Yes, it is.

Think!

What do you have in your room?

Listen, point, and say.

orange

black

purple

pink

Find the key words in the text. Then write them in your picture dictionary.

Understand

A Read *Max's Room* again. Choose ✔ or ✘.

1. The color words tell the color of things in the picture.

2. The color words tell how many.

3. The color words tell when.

Remember!
Color words tell what color things are.

B Choose the correct answer.

1. Max's room is **black /** ⟨**orange**⟩.

2. He has a **black / purple** plane.

3. He has a **pink / purple** kite.

C Complete the sentences.

| pink | orange | black | purple |

1.

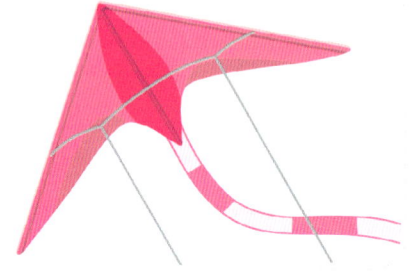

This is a ___pink___ kite.

2.

It's a _____ plane.

3.

This is an _____ room.

4.

It's a _____ backpack.

D Read *Max's Room* again. Look for the questions and answers. Complete the diagram.

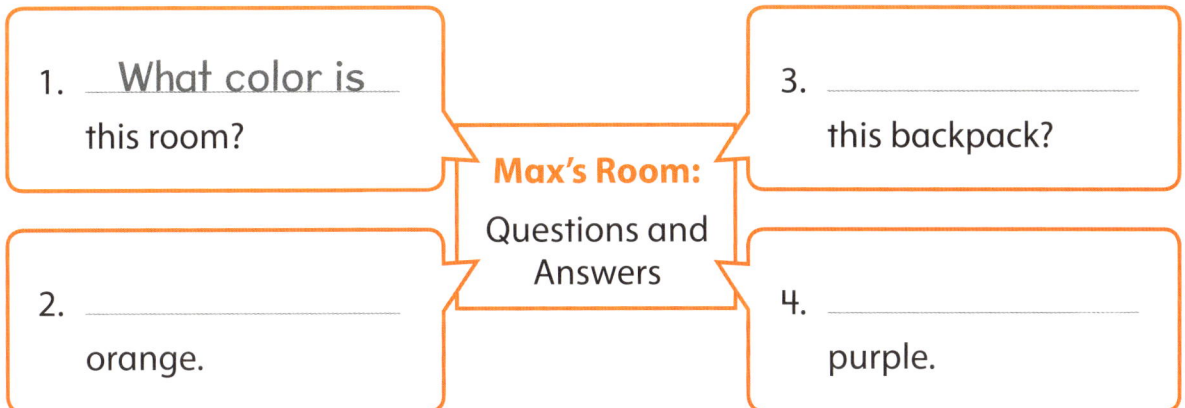

1. _What color is_ this room?

2. _____ orange.

Max's Room: Questions and Answers

3. _____ this backpack?

4. _____ purple.

E Look at **D**. Write. Use *What color is* or *It's*.

1.

What color is this ball?

It's orange.

2.

What color is this bike?

_____ black.

3.

_____ this door?

It's yellow.

4.

What color is this notebook?

_____ pink.

MY READING GOALS

☐ I can read the text.

☐ I can find the color words when I read. They tell what color things are.

Get Ready to Read

READING GOAL: Find the Shape Words
Words like *triangle*, *oval*, and *square* are shape words. Find the shape words when you read. They tell what things look like.

A Look at the pictures. What do they show? Choose ✔ or ✗.

1.
a shape

2.
a color

3.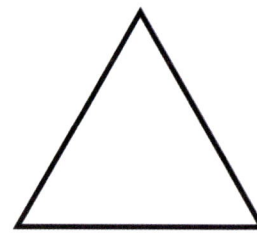
a color

B Read and listen. 🔊 19

This is a **shape word**.

Circles and Squares

Abby plays. She sees lots of shapes. She is on a step. It's a circle. She sees a sandbox. It's a square.

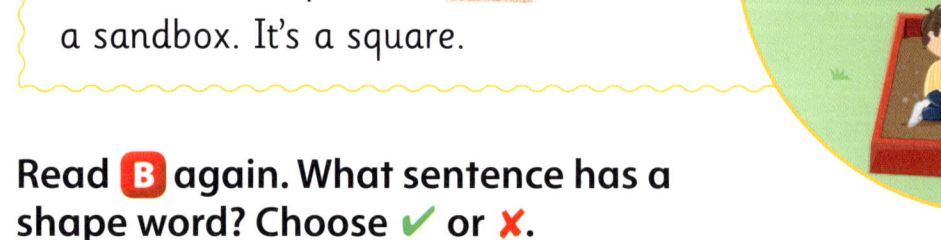

C Read **B** again. What sentence has a shape word? Choose ✔ or ✗.

1. Abby plays.
2. She sees a sandbox.
3. It's a square.

Read 🔊 20

Find the **shape words** in the story.

Shapes at the Park

"He has a kite. It's a rectangle," says Sing.

"Yes!" says Mrs. Hall.

"She has a balloon," says Sue. "It's a blue oval."

"Good!" says Mrs. Hall.

"Look at that balloon," says Sing. "Is it a heart?"

"Yes," says Mrs. Hall.

"Look!" says Sue. "This is a triangle."

Think!

What shapes do you see in your classroom?

Key Words 🔊 21

Listen, point, and say.

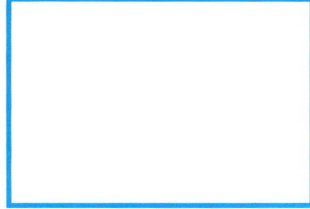

rectangle

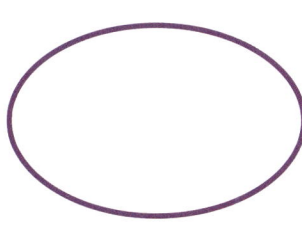

oval

heart

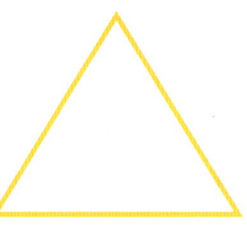

triangle

Find the key words in the story. Then write them in your picture dictionary.

Understand

Remember!
Shape words tell what things look like.

A Read *Shapes at the Park* again. Choose **Yes** or **No.**

1. The shape words tell about kites and balloons.   **Yes   No**

2. *Blue* is a shape word.   **Yes   No**

3. A heart is a shape.   **Yes   No**

B Choose the correct answer.

1. What shape is Sue's kite?

☐ a. a rectangle   ☑ b. a triangle

2. What shape is the girl's balloon?

☐ a. an oval   ☐ b. a rectangle

3. What shape is the boy's balloon?

☐ a. an oval   ☐ b. a heart

C Complete the sentences with key words. Then match.

1. Sue has a kite. It's a ___triangle.___

2. A boy has a kite. It's a _____

3. A boy has a balloon. It's a _____

4. The blue balloon is an _____

a.    b.    c.    d.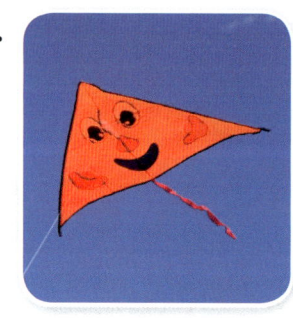

_____   _____   _____   ___1___

D A statement tells about something. It ends with a period (.).
A question asks about something. It ends with a question mark (?).
Complete the diagram.

	Question	Statement
1. It's a rectangle.		✔
2. Is it a heart?		
3. This is a triangle.		

E Look at **D**. Write. Use ? or .

1.

This is a heart __.__

2.

Is it a triangle ___

3.

Is it an oval ___

4.

It's a blue rectangle ___

MY READING GOALS

☐ I can read the story.

☐ I can find the shape words. They tell what things look like.

Reading Check

Remember!
Find the **color words**.
What colors are things?
Find the **shape words**. What do the things look like?

A **Read and listen.** 🔊 22

Avtar's House

This house has lots of colors and shapes. It has a TV. It's a black rectangle.

It has a door. It's an orange oval.

This is a heart. It's a poster. It's purple.

This is a cupboard. It's pink. The cupboard has a door. It's a pink triangle!

B **Find the color word *purple*. What is purple? Choose ✔ or ✘.**

1. a cupboard   ✘

2. a door   ✔ ✘

3. a poster   ✘

C Find the shape word *triangle*. What looks like a triangle? Choose ✔ or ✘.

1. a poster   ✔   ✘

2. a TV   ✔   ✘

3. a door   ✔   ✘

D Choose the correct answer.

1. What color is the TV?   purple   (black)

2. What color is the door?   orange   blue

3. What shape is the poster?   a heart   a rectangle

4. What shape is the TV?   a rectangle   a triangle

5. What color is the cupboard?   red   pink

E Complete the sentences.

orange	black	purple	pink
triangle	heart	oval	rectangle

1. The door is ____orange.____ (color)

2. The door is an _____ (shape)

3. The cupboard is _____ (color)

4. The cupboard door is a _____ (shape)

5. The poster is _____ (color)

6. The poster is a _____ (shape)

7. The TV is _____ (color)

8. The TV is a _____ (shape)

Get Ready to Write

WRITING GOAL: Write a Description

A description tells what something looks like. You can write descriptions of people, places, or things.

A Read the description. Underline the color word.

Writing Tip
Use color words in your descriptions.

This is my kitchen. It has orange cupboards. They're rectangles.

B Look at **A**. What words tell about the cupboards? Complete the diagram.

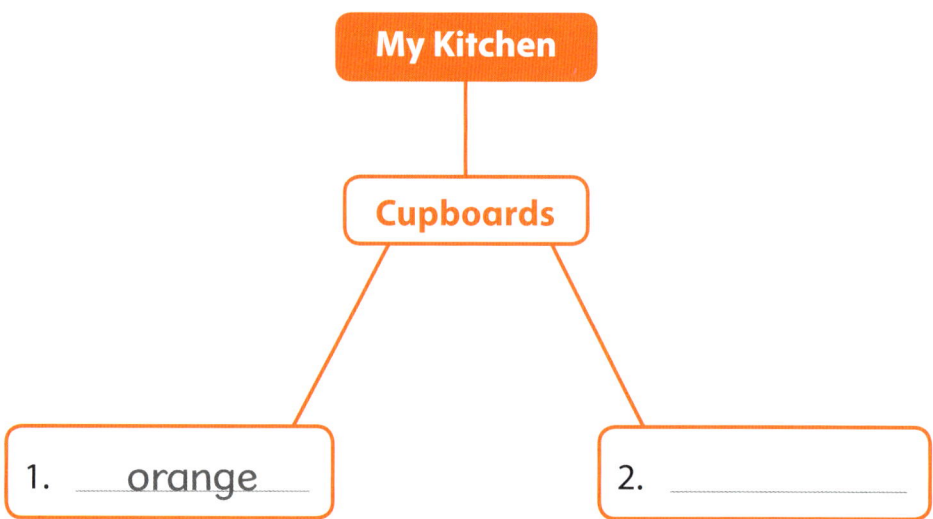

My Kitchen

Cupboards

1. _____orange_____

2. _____

Write

C Think about a room in your house. Complete the diagram.

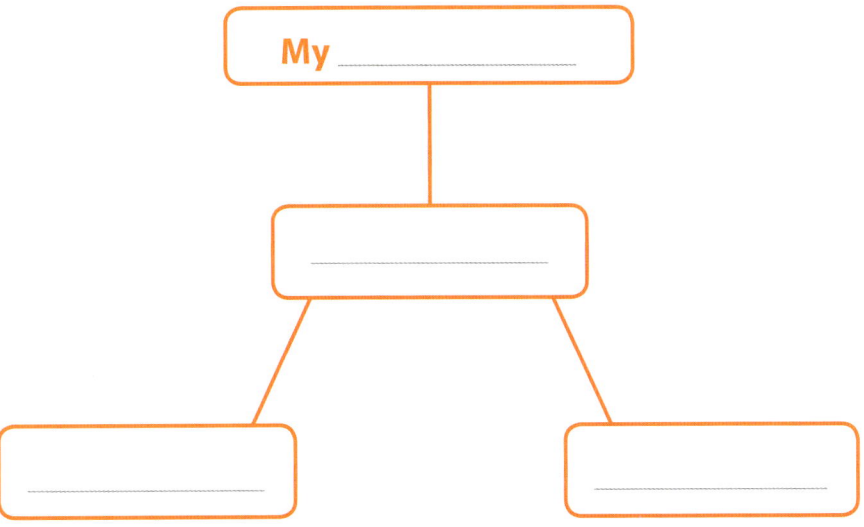

D Now write a description. Use your words from **C**. Choose new words, too. Then draw the room.

This is my _____.

It has _____ _____.

They're _____.

Now write a description of a different room.

MY WRITING GOAL

☐ I can write a description.

TOPIC 4

SOCIAL STUDIES

What Do You Like?

MY GOALS

UNIT 7
- Read the story *Goodbye, Mam!*
- Find the topic

UNIT 8
- Read the conversation *What Do You Want?*
- Find the details

WRITE
- Write a friendly letter

A Look at the picture. What do you see?
1. What are they doing?
2. How do they feel?

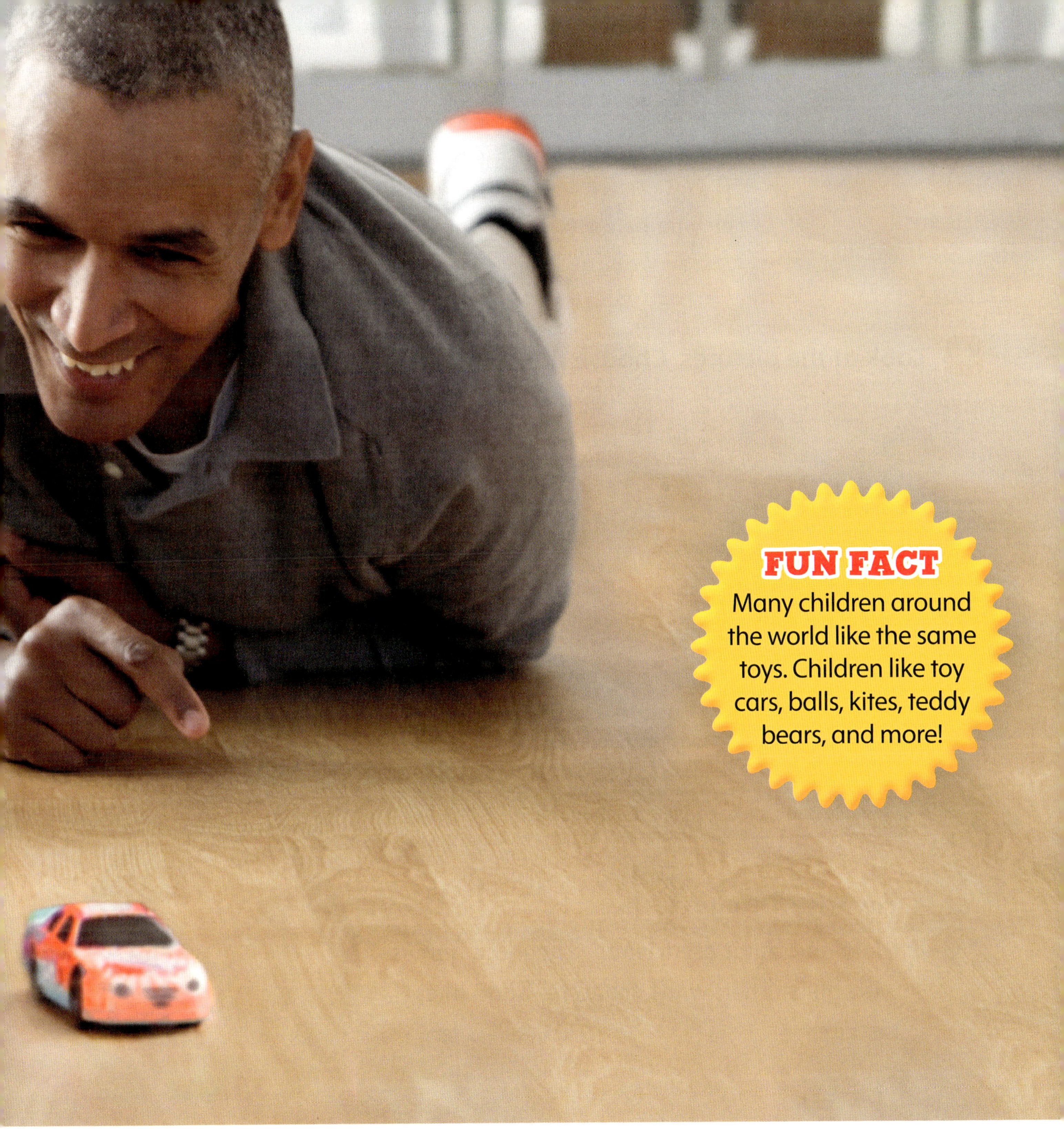

FUN FACT
Many children around the world like the same toys. Children like toy cars, balls, kites, teddy bears, and more!

B **Read the Fun Fact. Then answer the questions.**

1. Do many children like the same toys?
2. Do you like toy cars, balls, kites, or teddy bears?

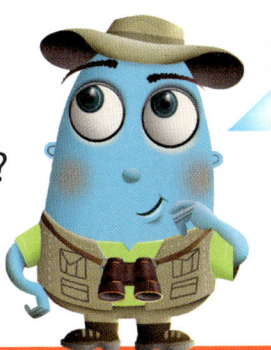

Think, Pair, Share
What do you do for fun?

Get Ready to Read

READING GOAL: Find the Topic
The topic is what the text is about. Look at the title and pictures before you read. They can tell you the topic.

A Look at the pictures. Choose the correct topic.

1.

☑ a. a good game
☐ b. my friend

2.

☐ a. toys at school
☐ b. toys at home

3.

☐ a. He learns to ride a bike.
☐ b. He learns to throw a ball.

B Read and listen. 23

The title and picture can tell you the **topic**.

Favorite Things

Matt and Sami are friends. They like games with balls. They want scooters! Sami likes his kite.

C Look at the title and picture again. What is the topic? Choose the correct answer.

☐ a. the boys
☐ b. what they like
☐ c. Sami's favorite toys

Read 🔊 24

What do you think the story is about?

Goodbye, Mam!

Mam has a new school. Mam's friends say goodbye.

She has a jump rope from Jack. It's red. She has a doll from Bella. She has a toy from Paul, too. It's a green robot.

"This is for you," says Ye-Won. "What is it?" asks Mam. "It's a yo-yo!" says Ye-Won.

Think!

Key Words 🔊 25

Listen, point, and say.

jump rope

doll

robot

yo-yo

Find the key words in the story. Then write them in your picture dictionary.

What toys do you like?

Understand

A Look at the title and picture. What is the topic? Choose the correct answer.

☐ a. Mam says goodbye. Her friends get toys.

☐ b. Mam's friends say goodbye. Mam gets toys.

B Choose the correct answer.

1. (Mam) / Ye-Won has a new school.

2. Mam has **four / five** toys.

3. The children are at **school / home**.

C Complete the sentences.

| yo-yo   robot   doll   jump rope |

1.

Mam has a ____yo-yo____
from Ye-Won.

2.

Mam has a _____
from Jack.

3.

She has a _____
from Bella.

4.

She has a _____
from Paul.

D Complete the diagram.

	It's a	It's
1. yo-yo	✔	
2. red		
3. doll		
4. gray		

E Look at **D**. Write *It's a* or *It's*.

1.

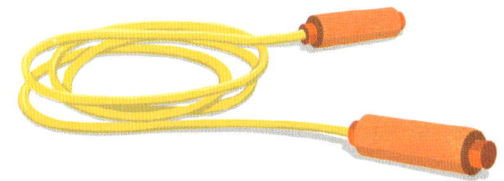

What is it?

____It's a____ jump rope.

2.

Do you have a doll?

Yes, I do. _____ brown.

3.

What is it?

_____ robot.

4.

What do you have?

I have a yo-yo. _____ blue.

MY READING GOALS

☐ I can read the story.   ☐ I can look at the title and pictures before I read. They can tell me the topic.

Get Ready to Read

READING GOAL: Find the Details

A detail is a word or sentence about the topic. It gives more information. Find the details when you read. They tell you more about the topic.

A Look at the picture. The words are details. What words tell about the train? Circle them.

little
new
toy
old
red
yellow
big

B Read and listen. 🔊 26

This is a **detail**.

Jen's Fruit Salad

Jen makes lots of fruit salads. Her mango fruit salad is great! It has two mangos. It has plums, too.

C Read **B** again. What is a detail? Choose ✔ or ✗.

1. Jen makes lots of fruit salads.   ✔   ✗

2. Jen likes fruit salad.   ✔   ✗

3. It has plums, too.   ✔   ✗

Read  🔊 27

What are the **details**? Underline them.

Listen, point, and say.

smoothie

juice

pizza

cake

What Do You Want?

Scott: Do you want a drink, Emma?

Emma: Yes, I do. I'm thirsty.

Scott: We have smoothies and juice. What do you want?

Emma: I want juice.

Scott: Are you hungry?

Emma: Yes, I am. I want pizza.

Scott: Do you want cake, too?

Emma: Yes, I do. I like cake.

Find the key words in the conversation. Then write them in your picture dictionary.

Think!

Do you like cake and juice? What do you eat with friends?

Understand

A Read *What Do You Want?* again. Choose **Yes** or **No**.

Remember!
The **details** tell you more about the topic.

1. The details tell about the food and drinks.   **Yes   No**

2. The details tell about Scott's friends.   **Yes   No**

3. The details tell what Scott likes.   **Yes   No**

B Choose the correct answer.

1. Where are Scott and Emma?
   - ✔ a. at Scott's house
   - ☐ b. at Emma's house

2. What do they have?
   - ☐ a. juice
   - ☐ b. water

3. What does Emma want?
   - ☐ a. a smoothie
   - ☐ b. juice

4. What does Emma like?
   - ☐ a. cake
   - ☐ b. smoothies

C Complete the sentences with key words. Then match.

1. The ___smoothie___ is purple.

2. She's thirsty. She wants apple _____.

3. He's hungry. He wants _____.

4. She doesn't want _____.

a.    b.    c.    d.
                                                                              1

D Read *What Do You Want?* again. Complete the diagram.
Work with a partner.

1. I'm _____hungry._____

4. I'm _____

2. I want
_____

3. I want
_____

5. I want
_____

6. I want
_____a smoothie._____

E Look at **D**. Write.

1.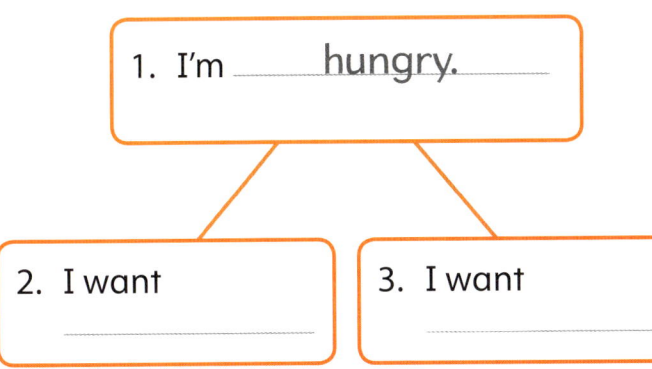

I'm hungry. I want _____pizza._____

2.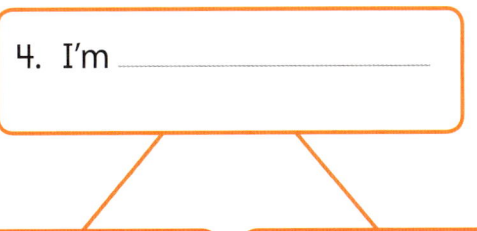

I'm _____ I want
_____

3.

Do you want _____
Yes, I do.

4.

Do you want _____
No, I don't.

MY READING GOALS

☐ I can read the
conversation.

☐ I can find the details when
I read. They tell me more
about the topic.

Reading Check

Remember!
Look at the title and pictures.
They help you find the **topic**.
Find the **details**. They tell
more about the topic.

A **Read and listen.** 29

What Do You Like?

Mary: Do you like my yo-yo?

Andy: Yes, I do. I have my robot.

Mary: Great! So, what do you want?

Andy: I want pizza.

Mary: I want cake. I'm thirsty, too.

Andy: Do you like smoothies?

Mary: Yes, I do. I want a fruit smoothie.

Andy: I like juice.

B **Look at the title and picture. What is the conversation about? Choose ✔ or ✘.**

1. favorite toys

2. pizza and cake

3. what to eat and drink

C Look at the conversation. What are some details? Choose ✔ or ✗.

1. Andy and Mary want pizza.   ✔ ☐   ✗ ☐

2. Mary is thirsty.   ✔ ☐   ✗ ☐

3. Mary likes fruit smoothies.   ✔ ☐   ✗ ☐

D Choose the correct answer.

1. Mary has a ____   ☐ a. robot.   ✔ b. yo-yo.

2. Andy has a ____   ☐ a. yo-yo.   ☐ b. robot.

3. Andy wants ____   ☐ a. pizza.   ☐ b. cake.

4. Mary wants ____   ☐ a. a fruit smoothie.   ☐ b. juice.

5. Andy likes ____   ☐ a. fruit smoothies.   ☐ b. juice.

E Unscramble and match.

1. y o - o y   • ———— •   a. I have this food for lunch. It has tomatoes.

     yo-yo

2. t o b o r   •   •   b. This toy is little.

3. i p z a z   •   •   c. You can make this drink from fruit and milk.

4. c e a k   •   •   d. You make this drink from fruit.

5. m s o e o t h i   •   •   e. This toy can have arms and legs.

6. u j i e c   •   •   f. I have this food with ice cream!

Get Ready to Write

WRITING GOAL: Write a Friendly Letter

A friendly letter is a letter to your friend or a family member. It has a greeting, such as *Dear Jane*. It has an ending, such as *Your friend*.

A Read the letter. Underline the commas.

Writing Tip
Use a comma after a greeting and an ending. Write your name after an ending.

Dear Suzie,

I have a red yo-yo. I have a blue jump rope, too. What toys do you like?

Your friend,

June

B Look at **A**. What is the greeting? What is the ending? Complete the diagram.

Friendly Letter

Greeting	Topic	Details	Ending
1. _____	2. my favorite toys	3. red yo-yo blue jump rope	4. _____

Write

C Think about your favorite toys. Complete the diagram.

Friendly Letter

Greeting	Topic	Details	Ending

D Now write a friendly letter. Use your words from **C**.
Choose new words, too. Then draw your favorite toys.

_____,

I have _____.

I have _____, too.

What toys do you like?

Your friend,

_____

Now write a letter to a friend about
some other toys.

MY WRITING GOAL

☐ I can write a friendly letter.

How's the Weather?

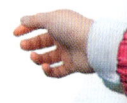

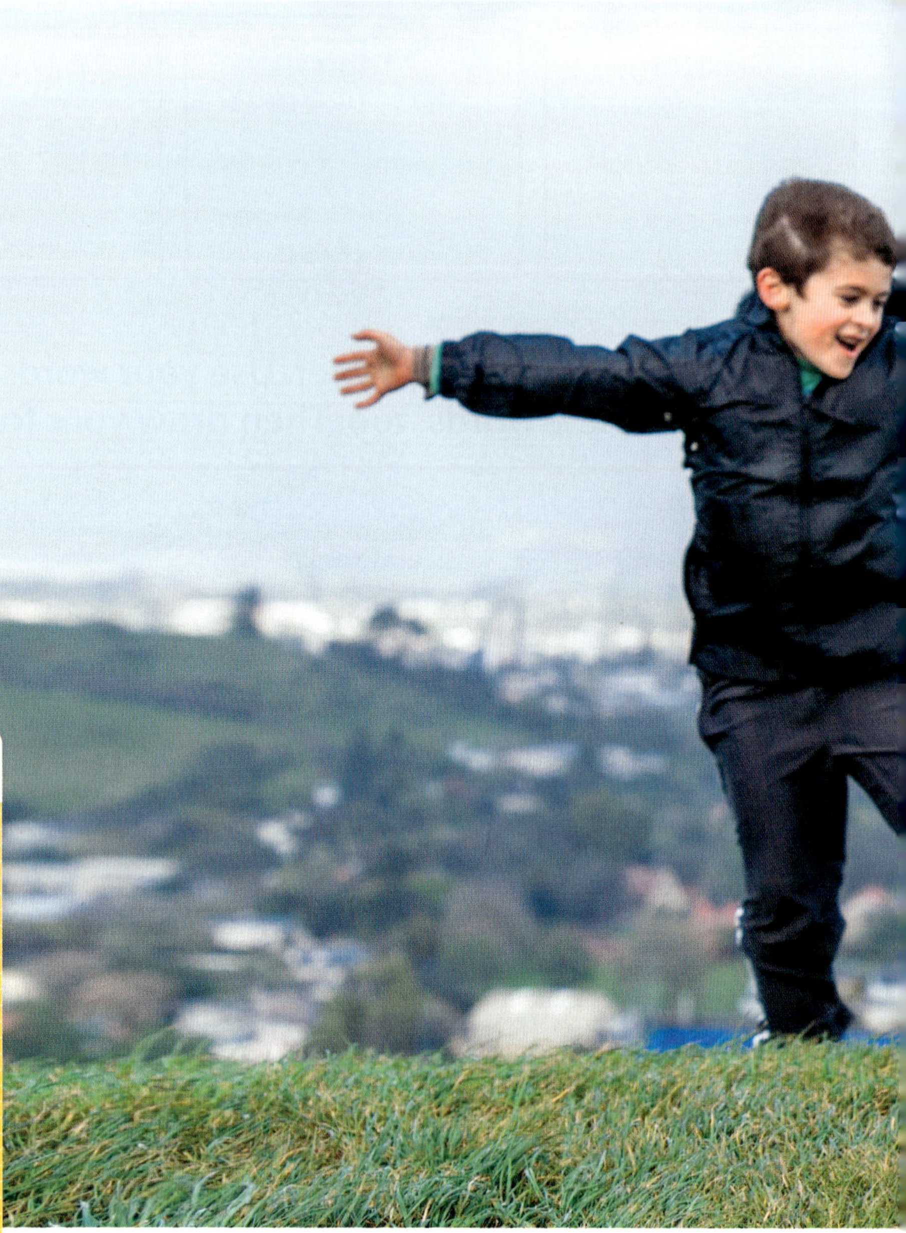

MY GOALS

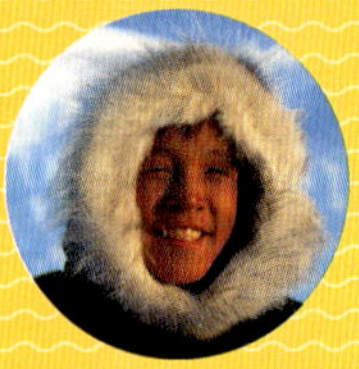

UNIT 9

- Read the text *Let's Learn about the Weather*
- Find the differences

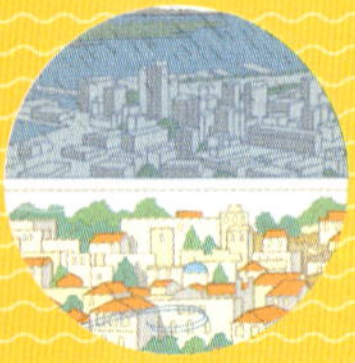

UNIT 10

- Read the story *Weather Talk*
- Find the cities

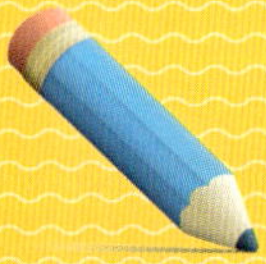

WRITE

- Write a weather report

A Look at the picture. What do you see?

1. How many children are there?
2. What are they doing?

FUN FACT

Wellington, New Zealand, gets lots of wind. The wind blows the trees and water. It isn't easy to walk!

B Read the Fun Fact. Then answer the questions.

1. What city gets lots of wind?
2. Do you have weather like this? When?

Think, Pair, Share
What's good weather?
What's bad weather?

Get Ready to Read

READING GOAL: Find the Differences

Differences show how things are not the same. For example, *new* and *old* are not the same. These words show differences. Find the differences when you read. They help you understand the text.

A Look at the pictures. What are the differences? Choose the correct answer.

1.

☑ a. big / little

☐ b. gray / white

2.

☐ a. new / old

☐ b. day / night

3.

☐ a. hungry / thirsty

☐ b. happy / sad

B Read and listen. 🔊 30

This is a **difference**.

The Seasons

The Earth has four seasons. They are spring, summer, fall, and winter. Some trees have leaves in the spring. They don't have leaves in the winter.

C Read **B** again. What is different? Choose the correct answer.

☐ a. the Earth

☐ b. the trees

☐ c. the winter

Read 31

What are the **differences**? Underline them.

Listen, point, and say.

cold

snowy

sunny

hot

www.studentsandscience.osw

Let's Learn about the Weather by Ava

Malik is from Greenland.

Ava: What's the weather like in Greenland?

Malik: It gets cold in the winter.

Ava: Does it snow?

Malik: Yes, it does. It's snowy. It doesn't snow in the summer.

Ava: How's the weather in the summer?

Malik: It's sunny. It doesn't get hot. It rains but not a lot.

Find the key words in the text. Then write them in your picture dictionary.

Think!

What's your weather like in the winter?

Understand

A Read *Let's Learn about the Weather* again. What's different? Choose the correct answer.

☐ a. the weather in the winter and the weather in the summer

☐ b. the weather in the winter and the weather today

B Choose the correct answer.

1. It **rains /** (**snows**) in the winter in Greenland.

2. It's **snowy / sunny** in the summer.

3. It **gets / doesn't get** hot in the summer.

C Complete the sentences.

hot	snowy	sunny	~~cold~~

1.

It gets _____cold_____ in the winter in Greenland.

2.

It's _____ in the winter.

3.

It's _____ in the summer.

4.

It doesn't get _____ in the summer.

D Read *Let's Learn about the Weather* again. Complete the diagram.

Weather	Summer	Winter
1. It gets cold.		✔
2. It doesn't snow.		
3. It doesn't get hot.		
4. It rains.		

E Look at **D**. Write. Use *gets*, *doesn't get, snows*, or *doesn't rain*.

1.

How's the weather in the spring?

It ____doesn't rain.____

2.

What's the weather like?

It _____ cold.

3.

How's the weather in the summer?

It _____ hot.

4.

What's the weather like in the winter?

It _____

MY READING GOALS

☐ I can read the text.

☐ I can find the differences. They help me understand the text.

Get Ready to Read

READING GOAL: Find the Cities

A city is a place with lots of people. A city is in a country. Names of cities start with a capital letter. Find the cities when you read. They tell you where things are.

A Look at the pictures. Are they cities? Choose ✔ or ✘.

1.    2.    3.

B Read and listen. 🔊 33

This is a **city**.

Two Cities

Ali is from Doha. It's in Qatar.
It's 45°C in the summer.
Vlad is from Omsk. It's in Russia.
It's about -22°C in the winter.

C Read **B** again. What are the cities? Choose ✔ or ✘.

1. Doha and Russia

2. Doha and Omsk

3. Omsk and Qatar

Read 🔊 34

Where are the **cities**? Underline them.

Weather Talk

Jane is from Auckland. It's a city in New Zealand. It's rainy today. In April and May, it's fall. It gets cloudy in the fall.

Jane's friend is Nikos. He's from Athens. It's a city in Greece. It's windy today. In April and May, it's spring. They don't get storms.

Think!

Key Words 🔊 35

Listen, point, and say.

rainy

cloudy

windy

storm

Find the key words in the story. Then write them in your picture dictionary.

What's your weather like today?

Understand

A Read *Weather Talk* again. Choose **Yes** or **No**.

1. Auckland is in New Zealand.   (Yes)   No

2. Jane is from Athens.   **Yes**   No

3. The cities have different
   weather today.   **Yes**   No

B Choose the correct answer.

1. Where is Nikos from?

   ☐ a. Auckland   ✔ b. Athens

2. Is it fall or spring in Auckland?

   ☐ a. fall   ☐ b. spring

3. Where is Athens?

   ☐ a. New Zealand   ☐ b. Greece

C Complete the sentences with key words. Then match.

1. It's ___windy___ today in Athens. She needs a hat.

2. Oh, no! The _____ has black clouds.

3. It's _____ today. We can't see the sun.

4. It's _____ in the city. Water is everywhere!

a.

b.

c.

d.

_____   _____   ____1____   _____

D Read *Weather Talk* again. Complete the diagram.

1. It's ___rainy___ today.

2. It gets _____ in the fall.

How's the weather?

3. It's _____ today.

4. They don't get _____ in the spring.

E Look at **D**. Write. Use an adjective or a noun.

1.

It's ___rainy___ today.

2.

It gets _____ in the fall.

3.

It's _____ today.

4.

They don't get _____ in the spring.

MY READING GOALS

☐ I can read the story.

☐ I can find the cities. They tell me where things are.

Reading Check

Remember!
Find the **differences**.
How are things not the
same? Find the **cities**.
Where are they?

 **A** **Read and listen.** 36

The Weather in New Delhi

Hello Uncle Pete,

I'm in New Delhi. It's a city in India. It's great!

It gets hot in the summer, but it's cold today. It isn't sunny. It's cloudy.

It's rainy and windy today. We have storms.

How's the weather in Rome? Is it cold, too?

Love,

Lisa

B **What is different? Choose ✔ or ✘.**

1. the weather in New Delhi and the weather in India ✔ ✘

2. the weather in the summer and the weather today ✔ ✘

3. the weather in New Delhi and the weather in Rome ✔ ✘

C Look at the cities. Where is Lisa? Choose ✔ or ✗.

1. Rome   ✔   ✗

2. home   ✔   ✗

3. New Delhi   ✔   ✗

D Choose the correct answer.

1. What's the weather like in New Delhi in the summer?   (hot)   cold

2. How's the weather in New Delhi today?   hot   cold

3. Is it sunny or cloudy in New Delhi today?   sunny   cloudy

4. Is it summer or winter in New Delhi?   summer   winter

5. Where is Uncle Pete?   New Delhi   Rome

6. Is Lisa happy or sad?   happy   sad

E Complete the sentences.

| cold | sunny | hot | rainy |
| cloudy | windy | storms | |

1. It's ___cloudy___ in New Delhi today. You can't see the sun.

2. It gets _____ in the summer.

3. They have _____ in New Delhi today.

4. It's _____ today. Oh, no! Can you catch my hat?

5. It's _____ in New Delhi today. Lisa has an umbrella.

6. It isn't hot. It's _____

7. It isn't _____ in New Delhi today.

Get Ready to Write

WRITING GOAL: Write a Weather Report

A weather report gives information about the weather.
It has words like *hot*, *cold*, *rainy*, or *windy*. It has pictures, too.

A Read the weather report. Underline the time words.

> **Writing Tip**
> Use time words in your weather report. Words like *Monday*, *weekend*, and *today* are time words.

Monday

I'm Maya Tan. This is the weather.
It's snowy today. It's cold and
windy, too.

B Look at **A**. What are the weather words? Complete the diagram.

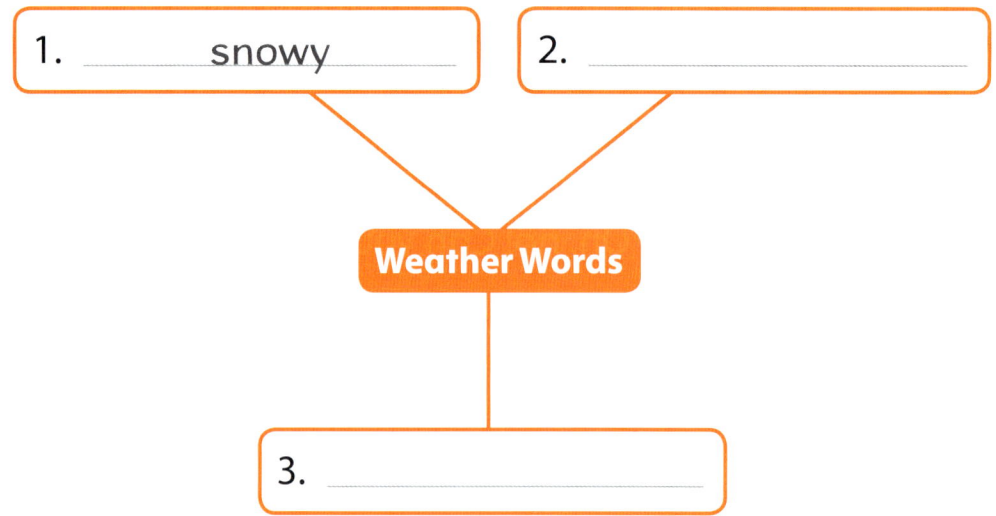

1. _____snowy_____

2. _____

Weather Words

3. _____

Write

C Think about your weather today. Complete the diagram.

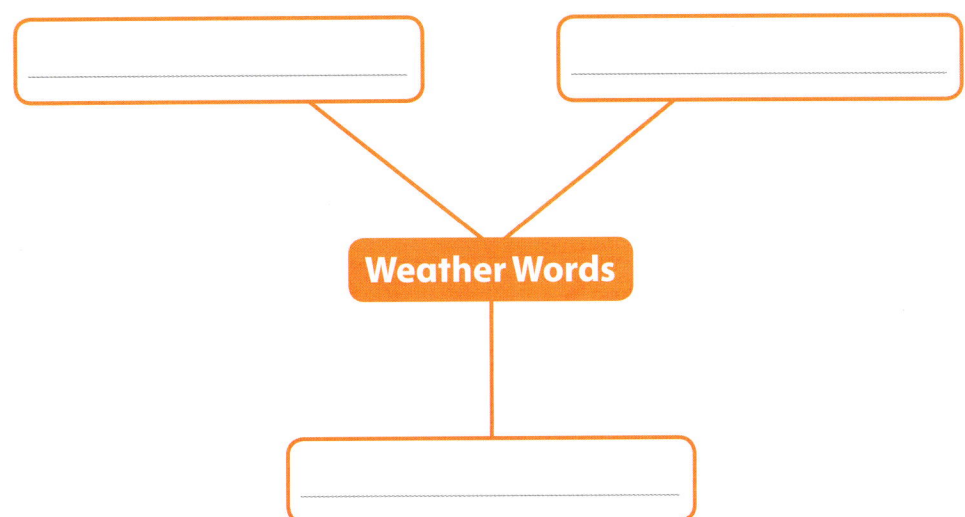

Weather Words

D Now write a weather report. Use your words from **C**. Choose new words, too. Then draw your weather.

_____

I'm _____. This is the

weather. It's _____ today.

It's _____ and

_____, too.

Now write a new weather report. Write about the weather in a different place.

MY WRITING GOAL

☐ I can write a weather report.

TOPIC 6

SOCIAL STUDIES

Family and Friends

MY GOALS

UNIT 11
- Read the story *Neighbors*
- Find the characters

UNIT 12
- Read the text *A New Classmate*
- Use a diagram

WRITE
- Write an autobiography

 Look at the picture. What do you see?

1. Where is the lion? Where is the snake?
2. Do you see families? Where?

FUN FACT

It's Chinese New Year! Children don't go to school. They have fun! Many people on Earth enjoy this day.

B Read the Fun Fact. Then answer the questions.

1. Do children go to school on this day?

2. What day do you like?

Think, Pair, Share
What do you do with your family?

Get Ready to Read

READING GOAL: Find the Characters
Characters are people or animals in a story. Their names start with a capital letter. Find the characters when you read to know who is in the story.

A Look at the picture. Who are the characters? Draw lines.

May
Jim
Tom

B Read and listen. 🔊 37

This is a **character**.

Two Cousins

City Mouse and Country Mouse are cousins. They have fruit and cookies. "Wow!" says Country Mouse. A man comes. "Run!" says City Mouse.

C Read **B** again. Who is in the story? Choose the correct answer.

- [ ] a. Country Mouse and a girl
- [ ] b. City Mouse, Country Mouse, and a man
- [ ] c. City Mouse and Country Mouse

Read 38

Who are the **characters**? Underline them.

Neighbors

Will meets a new girl, Kay.

"Is he your father?" asks Will.

"Yes," says Kay. "And she's my mother."

"Who's this?"

"She's Tia," says Kay. "She's my baby sister. She's thirsty."

"Who's he?"

"He's Phil," says Kay. "He's my brother."

"Well, goodbye," says Will.

"Goodbye," says Kay. "It's nice to meet you!"

Listen, point, and say.

father

mother

baby sister

brother

Find the key words in the story. Then write them in your picture dictionary.

Think!

Do you have brothers or sisters? What are their names?

Understand

A Read *Neighbors* again. Who is in the story? Choose the correct answer.

Remember!
The **characters** are the people in the story.

☐ a. Kay, Will, and Will's family

☐ b. Kay, Will, and Kay's family

B Choose the correct answer.

1. Kay talks about her **friends / ⟨family⟩**.

2. Phil is Kay's **father / brother**.

3. Kay has a baby **brother / sister**.

C Complete the sentences.

| father | ~~baby sister~~ | mother | brother |

1.

Kay's _baby sister_ is thirsty.

2.

Kay's _____ makes a salad.

3.

Kay's _____ is hungry.

4.

Kay's _____ gets drinks.

D Read *Neighbors* again. Who are the people? Complete the diagram.

He's

1. _father_   2. _____

She's

3. _____   4. _____

E Look at **D**. Write. Use *She's* or *He's*.

1.

_He's_ my _father_

2.

_____ my _____

3.

_____ my _____

4.

_____ my _____

MY READING GOALS

☐ I can read the story.   ☐ I can find the characters when I read. Then I know who is in the story.

Get Ready to Read

READING GOAL: Use a Diagram
A diagram is a picture. It shows important information. Look at the diagrams when you read. They help you understand a text.

A Look at the diagram. Match the pictures with the people.

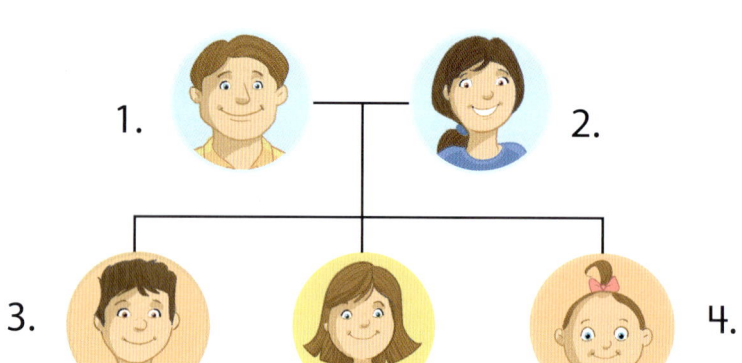

1.   2.

3.   4.

me

baby sister	___
father	1
brother	___
mother	___

B Read and listen. 🔊 40

This is a **diagram**.

A Family Tree

I'm Jouri. This is Manar. She's my baby sister. This is my mother. This is my father. These are my grandparents.

C Read **B** again. What does the diagram show? Choose ✔ or ✗.

1. Jouri's family   ✗

2. Jouri's classmates   ✔ ✗

3. Jouri's friends   ✔ ✗

Read 41

Look at the **diagram**. What does it show?

A New Classmate

Mi-Na is from Seoul. It's a city in South Korea.

Mi-Na: This is my family.

Chris: Who's she?

Mi-Na: She's my aunt. She's fun!

Chris: Is she your sister?

Mi-Na: Ji-Ho? Yes, she is. And this is my grandmother. She likes animals.

Chris: Who's this?

Mi-Na: He's my grandfather. He's 98 years old!

Sun-Ja   Young-Sik

Ha-Na

Ji-Sun

Sung-Min

Mi-Na

Ji-Ho

Think!

Think about your family. What do they like?

Key Words 42

Listen, point, and say.

aunt

sister

grandmother

grandfather

Find the key words in the text. Then write them in your picture dictionary.

Understand

Remember!
A **diagram** helps us understand a text.

A Read *A New Classmate* again. Choose **Yes** or **No**.

1. The diagram shows Mi-Na's family.   **Yes**   **No**
2. Sun-Ja is Mi-Na's grandmother.   **Yes**   **No**
3. Mi-Na has a brother.   **Yes**   **No**

B Choose the correct answer.

1. Who is Ha-Na?
   - ☐ a. Mi-Na's sister
   - ☑ b. Mi-Na's aunt
2. Who is Mi-Na's father?
   - ☐ a. Sung-Min
   - ☐ b. Young-Sik
3. Who is Ji-Ho's mother?
   - ☐ a. Ji-Sun
   - ☐ b. Ha-Na
4. Who is very old?
   - ☐ a. Mi-Na's aunt
   - ☐ b. Mi-Na's grandfather

C Complete the sentences with key words. Then match.

1. Ji-Ho is Mi-Na's _____sister._____

2. Mi-Na's _____ is 98 years old.

3. Mi-Na's _____ is fun.

4. Mi-Na's _____ likes animals.

a.    b.    c.    d.

_____1_____   _____   _____   _____

D Read *A New Classmate* again. Look for the questions and answers. Complete the diagram.

Questions

Answers

1. <u>Who's she?</u> → She's my aunt.

2. _____ your sister? → Yes, she is.

E Look at **D**. Write. Use *Who's she / he* or *Is she / he.*

1.

<u>Who's she?</u>
She's my aunt.

2.

_____
He's my grandfather.

3.

_____ your grandmother?
Yes, she is.

4.

_____ your sister?
No, she isn't. She's my cousin.

MY READING GOALS

☐ I can read the text.

☐ I can use a diagram. It helps me understand the text.

Reading Check

> **Remember!**
> Find the **characters**.
> Who is in the story?
> Look at the **diagrams**.
> What do they show?

A Read and listen.  43

Aunt Chi

Who's this? Aunt Chi! She's from Hanoi. It's a city in Vietnam. She's at Lan's house!

Lan looks at her mother. She's happy. Lan looks at her father. He's happy.

"Hi!" says Lan. "I'm Lan! He's my brother. She's my baby sister."

"She's big!" says Aunt Chi. "It's nice to meet you!"

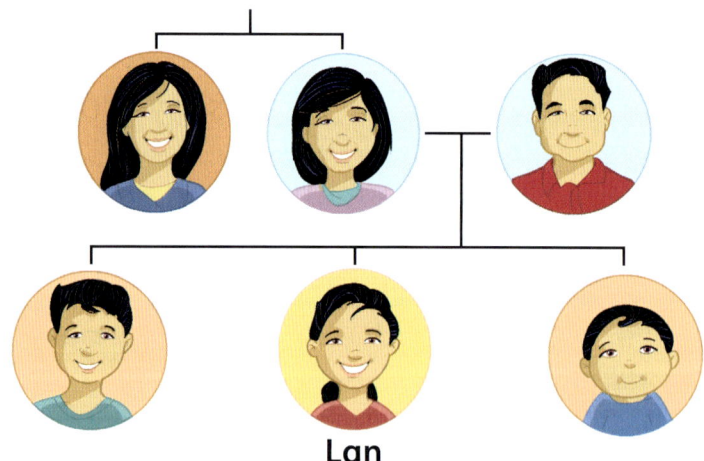

Lan

B Find the characters. Who are they? Choose ✔ or ✗.

1. Aunt Chi and her friends

2. Aunt Chi and her cousins

3. Aunt Chi and Lan's family

C Look at the diagram. What does it show? Choose ✔ or ✘.

1. Lan has two sisters.   ✔   ✘

2. Lan's mother and Aunt Chi are sisters.   ✔   ✘

3. Lan's father has an aunt.   ✔   ✘

D Choose the correct answer.

1. Who is from Hanoi?   ✔ a. Lan's aunt   ☐ b. Lan's father

2. Where is the family?   ☐ a. at Lan's house   ☐ b. in Hanoi

3. Is Lan's mother happy?   ☐ a. Yes, she is.   ☐ b. No, she isn't.

4. How many children
   are there?   ☐ a. two   ☐ b. three

E Unscramble and match.

1. s i t r s e   •   • a. This is a dad.

   sister

2. m t r o h e   •   • b. This child is a girl.

   _____

3. a t u n   •   • c. She's my mother's sister.

   _____

4. f a t r h e   •   • d. This child is a boy.

   _____

5. b y a b s i t r e s •   • e. This is a mom.

   _____

6. h b r o r t e   •   • f. This girl is very young.

   _____

Get Ready to Write

WRITING GOAL: Write an Autobiography

An autobiography is a story about your life. It has your name. It tells where you are from. It gives other information about you.

A Read the autobiography. Who is it about? Underline the name.

Writing Tip
Use *I* and *my* to write about your life.

My name is Luke. I'm from Paris. I like games and music.

B Look at **A**. What is the information? Complete the diagram.

My Autobiography

My name	**I'm from**	**I like**
1. ___Luke___	2. _____	3. _____

Write

C Think about your life. Complete the diagram.

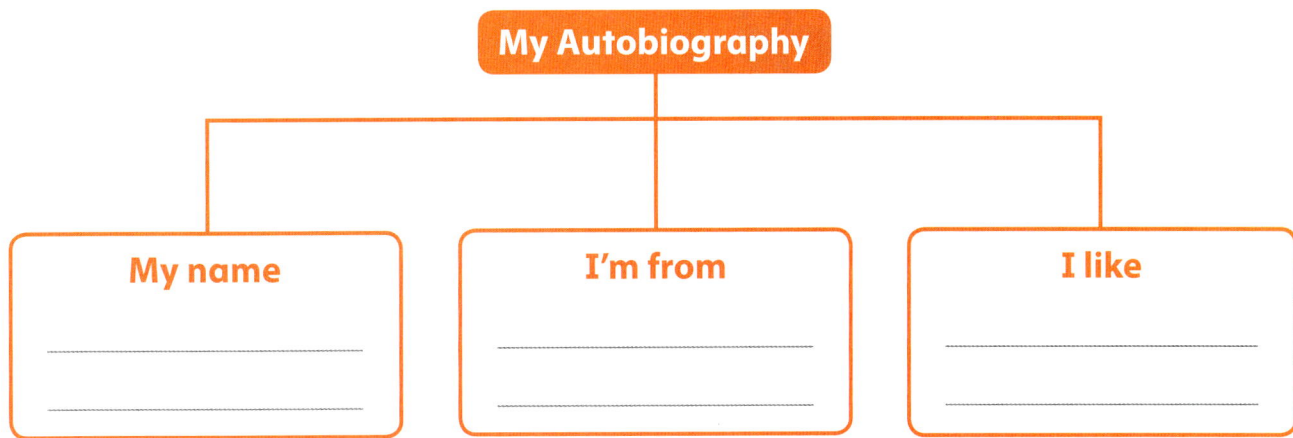

My Autobiography

My name	I'm from	I like
_____ _____	_____ _____	_____ _____

D Now write your autobiography. Use your words from **C**.
Choose new words, too. Then draw your family.

My name is _____. I'm from _____.
I like _____ and _____.

Now pretend to be someone else. Choose a friend or a
person from your family. Write an autobiography.

MY WRITING GOAL

☐ I can write an autobiography.

Reading
WITH Writing
1

Workbook

Sarah Jane Lewis-Mantzaris

OXFORD
UNIVERSITY PRESS

Read

READING GOAL:
Look at the Pictures

Remember!
Pictures show what a text is about.

A Where is the picture? Circle it.

TO: Eva   **FROM:** Tom

SUBJECT: My Classroom

Hi Eva!

This is my classroom. This is my teacher. I have a desk. I have a chair. I have a wastebasket, too.

Do you have a backpack? I have two books in my backpack.

There's a bookcase. There's a fish! Do you have a fish? What do you have in your classroom?

Tom

B Read the text. Then choose the correct answer.

1. What does Tom have?
   ☑ a. a desk   ☐ b. a pencil case   ☐ c. a pen

2. What is in the classroom?
   ☐ a. posters   ☐ b. a wastebasket   ☐ c. a cupboard

3. What is in the backpack?
   ☐ a. a pencil case   ☐ b. pens   ☐ c. books

4. What is the picture about?
   ☐ a. Tom's books   ☐ b. Tom's classroom   ☐ c. Tom's backpack

C Trace the words. Then choose the correct picture.

1. chair

☐ a.   ✔ b.

2. desk

☐ a.   ☐ b.

3. bookcase

☐ a.   ☐ b.

4. wastebasket

☐ a.   ☐ b.

D Complete the sentences.

| wastebasket | ~~bookcase~~ | chair | desk |

1. The books are in the bookcase.

2. I sit on that _____

3. I put old papers in the _____

4. I write at my _____

E Unscramble and write.

1. o b o k s e c a

   bookcase

2. w s a t e b k s a t e

   _____

3. k s e d

4. h a c r i

   _____

Read

READING GOAL:
Find the Numbers

Remember!
Numbers tell how many.

A Read. Think about the numbers.

Find the Things

"What do you have?" asks Liam.

"I have a pencil case," says Ji-Su.
"I have two pens. I have three crayons.
But I can't find the markers."

"Is this a marker?" asks Liam.

"Yes, it is," says Ji-Su.

"Great!" says Liam. "I have four markers!"

B Read again. Then choose the correct answer.

1. Ji-Su has a pencil case.   (Yes)   No
2. She has two pencils.   Yes   No
3. Ji-Su has five crayons.   Yes   No
4. Liam has four markers. Four is a number.   Yes   No

C Complete the sentences.

| pencils | markers | crayons | pencil case |

1.

   I have two ___pencils.___

2.

   These are my _____

3.

   I have six _____

4.

   This is my _____

D Complete the sentences.

1. I have four pens in my _pencil case._

2. I draw with a _p_____, not a pen.

3. My teacher writes with a _m_____ in my book.

4. I color with _c_____

Write

Remember!
Start a sentence with a capital letter. End a sentence with a period.

Circle the capital letters and periods.

Grace: Is this a crayon?

Dan: No, it isn't. It's a pen.

Read

READING GOAL:
Read the Title

A Where is the title? Underline it.

Great Pets: Hamsters

Hamsters are great pets. They're clean. They're little and fun.

Turtles and frogs can't run. They can't play. Can hamsters play? Yes, they can. Can they run? Yes, they can.

Birds can talk. Can hamsters talk? No, they can't. But they can learn their names!

B Read. Then choose the correct answer.

1. What animals can play?
   ☐ a. turtles   ☐ b. frogs   ☑ c. hamsters

2. What animals can talk?
   ☐ a. birds   ☐ b. turtles   ☐ c. hamsters

3. What can hamsters do?
   ☐ a. talk   ☐ b. run   ☐ c. fly

4. Read the title again. What is the text about?
   ☐ a. pets   ☐ b. big pets   ☐ c. pet hamsters

C Trace the words. Then choose the correct picture for each word.

1. _____bird_____

☐ a.   ☑ b.

2. _____cat_____

☐ a.   ☐ b.

3. _____hamster_____

☐ a.   ☐ b.

4. _____dog_____

☐ a.   ☐ b.

D Complete the sentences.

bird	dog	hamster	cat

1. A ____cat____ sleeps a lot.

2. A _____ can help.

3. A _____ can talk.

4. A _____ can learn its name.

E Unscramble and write.

1. atc

_____cat_____

2. bdir

_____

3. odg

_____

4. armhste

_____

Read

READING GOAL:
Read the Captions

A Read. Look at the picture and caption.

At the Zoo

Zoe and Joe are at the zoo.

"I like turtles," says Joe. "I don't like frogs."

"I like horses," says Zoe. "I don't like rabbits."

"Look at the birds," says Joe. "They're big!"

"Hello! Can you talk?" asks Zoe. "Yes, I can," says a bird. Joe laughs.

"My name is Munya!"

B Read again. Then choose the correct answer.

1. Does Joe like frogs?   **Yes**   (**No**)
2. Does Zoe like rabbits?   **Yes**   **No**
3. Are the birds little?   **Yes**   **No**
4. Can the bird talk?   **Yes**   **No**
5. Does Joe laugh?   **Yes**   **No**
6. Is Munya a bird?   **Yes**   **No**

C Complete the sentences.

| rabbit | ~~frog~~ | horse | turtle |

1.

A ____frog____ can jump.

2.

A _____ is little.

3.

A _____ can't run.

4.

You can ride a _____

D Complete the sentences.

1. A __horse____ is big.

2. A f_____ is little.

3. A t_____ can't play.

4. A r_____ can jump.

Write

Circle the correct caption.

Horses can play.

You can ride a horse.

Remember!
A picture and a caption give more information.

Read

READING GOAL:
Find the Color Words

A Read. Look for the color words.

We Can Make Colors

Look at the picture. It has lots of colors.
We can make colors!

Red and blue make purple.
This is my purple backpack.

Yellow and red make orange.
It's an orange room.

Red and white make pink.
Is this a pink kite?
Yes, it is.

B Read again. Then choose the correct answer.

1. What color is the backpack?
   - ✔ a. purple ☐ b. red ☐ c. blue
2. What colors make orange?
   - ☐ a. red and blue ☐ b. yellow and red ☐ c. red and white
3. What colors make pink?
   - ☐ a. red and blue ☐ b. yellow and red ☐ c. red and white
4. How many color words are in the text?
   - ☐ a. six ☐ b. eight ☐ c. twelve

C Trace the words. Then choose the correct picture for each word.

1. black

☑ a.   ☐ b.

2. pink

☐ a.   ☐ b.

3. purple

☐ a.   ☐ b.

4. orange

☐ a.   ☐ b.

D Complete the sentences.

purple	~~orange~~	pink	black

1. It's an ___orange___ room.

2. It's a _____ kite.

3. It's a _____ backpack.

4. It's a _____ plane.

E Unscramble and write.

1. prepul

___purple___

2. lbakc

_____

3. roaeng

4. pkin

_____

Read

READING GOAL:
Find the Shape Words

A Read. Look for the shape words.

A Game

Riko has a balloon. "What shape is this?" she asks.

"Is it a triangle?" asks Loc.

"No, it's a heart."

Loc has a book. "What shape is this?" he asks.

"Is it a rectangle?" asks Riko.

"Yes, it is."

"This is an oval," says Riko.

Where is the oval?

B Read again. Then choose the correct answer.

1. Is the balloon a triangle?   **Yes**   (**No**)
2. Is the book a rectangle?   **Yes**   **No**
3. Is the backpack a heart?   **Yes**   **No**
4. Is *oval* a shape word?   **Yes**   **No**

C Complete the sentences.

| heart | triangle | oval | rectangle |

1.

This is an ____oval.____

2.

It's a _____

3.

This is a _____

4.

It's a _____

D Complete the sentences.

1. I have a __heart_____ on my notebook.

2. My book is a _r_____

3. This poster is a _t_____

4. I have an _o_____ on my backpack.

Write

Circle the color words.

This is my room. It has blue walls. They're rectangles. It has a yellow poster. It's a heart.

> **Remember!** Use color words in your descriptions.

Read

READING GOAL:
Find the Topic

Remember!
The **topic** is what the text is about.

A Can you find the topic? Underline it.

The Robot

I want a robot.

I don't want a doll.

I have a good yo-yo,

A jump rope, and ball.

I want a green robot.

A robot that goes!

What is it? A robot?

I don't know.

B Read. Then choose the correct answer.

1. What does the child want?
   - ✔ a. a robot
   - ☐ b. a doll
   - ☐ c. a jump rope

2. What doesn't the child want?
   - ☐ a. a yo-yo
   - ☐ b. a jump rope
   - ☐ c. a doll

3. What is green?
   - ☐ a. the jump rope
   - ☐ b. the robot
   - ☐ c. the yo-yo

4. What is the poem about?
   - ☐ a. food
   - ☐ b. a toy
   - ☐ c. colors

C Trace the words. Then choose the correct picture for each word.

1. doll

☑ a.　　　☐ b.

2. yo-yo

☐ a.　　　☐ b.

3. robot

☐ a.　　　☐ b.

4. jump rope

☐ a.　　　☐ b.

D Complete the sentences.

| doll | ~~robot~~ | yo-yo | jump rope |

1. I have a green ____robot____. It can walk!

2. I have a _____ in my backpack.

3. This is my _____. It has brown hair.

4. A _____ is a little toy.

E Unscramble and write.

1. ujpm reop

____jump rope____

2. yo-oy

_____

3. rotbo

_____

4. ldol

_____

Read

READING GOAL:
Find the Details

Remember!
The **details** tell you more about the topic.

A Read. Look for the details.

Dear Ruby,

Thank you for your letter. What do I do? I make pizza. Pizza is my favorite food!

I like cake, too. I like juice. I don't like smoothies.

Please come with your family. You can eat my pizza!

Your friend,

Adam

B Read again. Then choose the correct answer.

1. Adam likes pizza.   (Yes)   No
2. Adam makes cakes.   Yes   No
3. Adam likes smoothies.   Yes   No
4. "Pizza is my favorite food" is a detail.   Yes   No

C Complete the sentences.

| pizza | ~~juice~~ | cake | smoothie |

1.

I want ___juice.___

2.

I don't want a _____

3.

I like _____

4.

She likes _____

D Complete the sentences.

1. I like ___cake___ and ice cream.

2. I have a fruit ___s___

3. I want orange ___j___

4. He likes ___p___ with tomatoes.

Write

Circle the greeting and the ending.

Hi Leah,

I like pizza. What's your favorite food?

Love,

Mia

Remember!
Use a comma after
greetings and endings.

Read

READING GOAL:
Find the Differences

Remember!
Differences show how things are not the same.

A Read. Think about the differences.

The Weather in June

This is Rome. It's a city in Italy. It's the summer. It gets hot in the summer. It's sunny. It rains but not a lot.

This is Perth. It's a city in Australia. It's the winter. It gets cold in the winter. It's windy. It isn't snowy.

B Read again. Then choose the correct answer.

1. What month is it?
   ☐ a. May   ☑ b. June   ☐ c. July

2. What's the weather like in Rome?
   ☐ a. It's windy and sunny.   ☐ b. It's cold and rainy.
   ☐ c. It's hot and sunny.

3. What's the weather like in Perth?
   ☐ a. It's hot and sunny.   ☐ b. It's cold and snowy.
   ☐ c. It's cold and windy.

4. What is different?
   ☐ a. Rome is hot and Perth is cold.   ☐ b. Perth is hot and Rome is cold.
   ☐ c. Rome is windy and Perth is sunny.

C Trace the words. Then choose the correct picture for each word.

1. _____ hot _____

☐ a.   ☑ b.

2. _____ sunny _____

☐ a.   ☐ b.

3. _____ cold _____

☐ a.   ☐ b.

4. _____ snowy _____

☐ a.   ☐ b.

D Complete the sentences.

| hot | snowy | cold | ~~sunny~~ |

1. It's ____sunny____ in Rome in June.

2. It gets _____ in the summer in Rome.

3. It gets _____ in the winter in Perth.

4. It isn't _____ in the winter in Perth.

E Unscramble and write.

1. nyosw

____snowy____

2. suynn

_____

3. dcol

_____

4. oth

_____

Read

READING GOAL:
Find the Cities

Remember!
Cities tell you
where things are.

A Read. Look for the city.

It's Snowy Today!

Omar and Hany are from Cairo. It's a city in Egypt.
It's hot in Cairo. It isn't very rainy. It's sunny.

It's the winter in Cairo. It's windy. It gets cloudy in
the winter, but it's different today! They have storms.
It's snowy. Omar and Hany love snow!

B Read again. Then choose the correct answer.

1. Is it cold a lot in Cairo?   **Yes**   (**No**)

2. Does it rain a lot?   **Yes**   **No**

3. Does it get cloudy in the winter?   **Yes**   **No**

4. Is Cairo a city?   **Yes**   **No**

C Complete the sentences.

storms	cloudy	rainy	windy

1.

It gets ___cloudy___ in Cairo in the winter.

2.

They have _____ today.

3.

It's _____ today in the story.

4.

It isn't very _____ in Cairo.

D Complete the sentences.

1. It's _cloudy_ today. I can't see the sun.

2. It's _r_____ today. I have my umbrella.

3. They have _s_____ in the winter.

4. It's _w_____ today. I have my jacket.

Write

Circle the time words.

Tuesday

I'm Molly. This is the weather. It's hot today. It's sunny and windy, too.

Remember!
Use time words in your weather report.

Read

READING GOAL:
Find the Characters

Remember!
The **characters** are the people in the story.

A Read. Look for the characters. Who are they?

At the Park

"Hi, Oscar," says Todd. "These are my parents."

"It's nice to meet you," says Oscar.

"It's nice to meet you, too," says Todd's mother. "Hi, Oscar!" says Todd's father.

"This is Owen. He's my brother. And this is Kate. She's my baby sister. Let's play, OK?"

"Yes!" says Oscar.

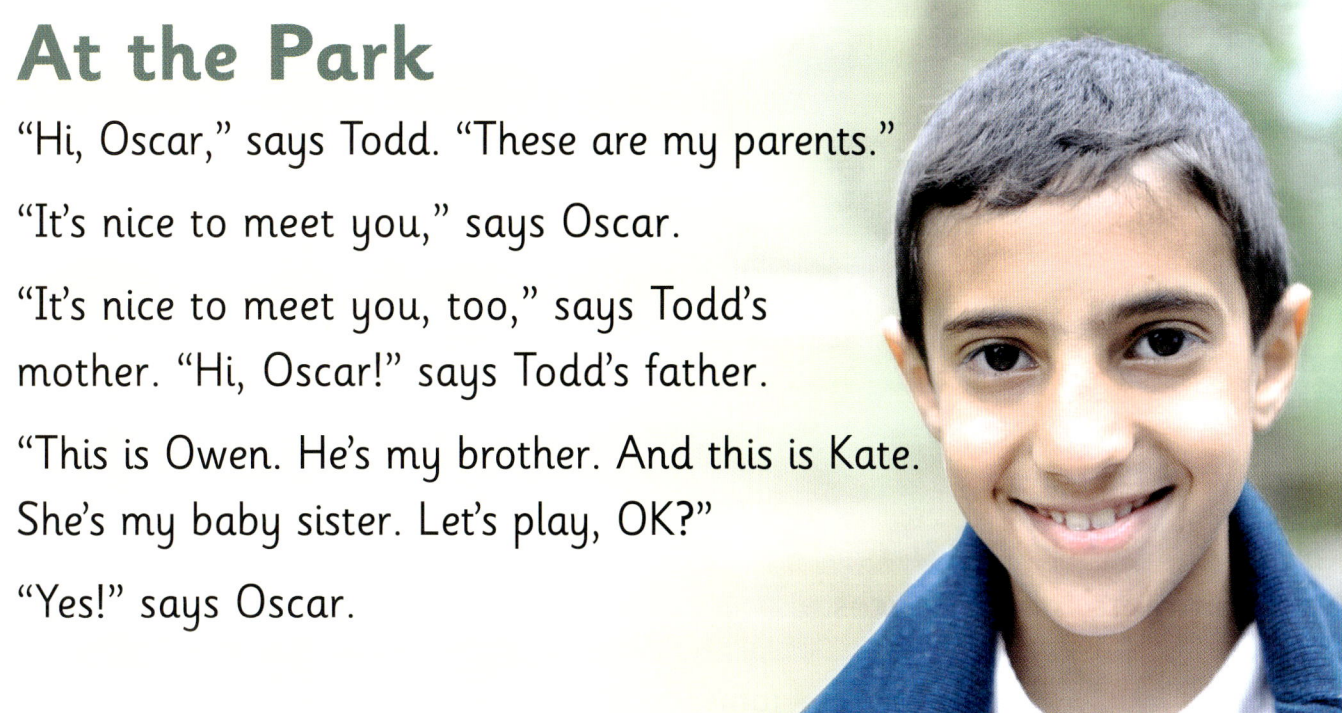

B Read again. Then choose the correct answer.

1. Who is Todd's friend?
   ☐ a. Owen   ☐ b. Kate   ✔ c. Oscar

2. Who is Owen?
   ☐ a. Todd's brother   ☐ b. Oscar's friend   ☐ c. Todd's father

3. Who is Kate?
   ☐ a. Todd's mother   ☐ b. Todd's baby sister
   ☐ c. Oscar's baby sister

4. Who are the characters?
   ☐ a. Todd and Oscar's family   ☐ b. Oscar and Todd's family
   ☐ c. Todd and his friends

C Trace the words. Then choose the correct picture for each word.

1. brother

☑ a.   ☐ b.

2. mother

☐ a.   ☐ b.

3. baby sister

☐ a.   ☐ b.

4. father

☐ a.   ☐ b.

D Complete the sentences.

| brother | father | baby sister | mother |

1. He's my _____brother_____. He's 14 years old.

2. This is my _____. She's little.

3. This is my _____. He's tall.

4. This is my _____. She likes music.

E Unscramble and write.

1. tmorhe

_____mother_____

2. ybab rsiste

_____

3. frahte

_____

4. rbotrhe

_____

WORKBOOK
UNIT
12

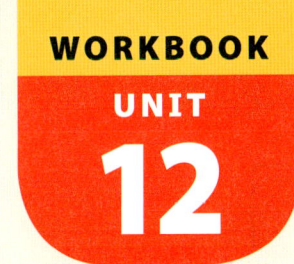

Read

READING GOAL:
Use a Diagram

Remember!
A **diagram** helps us understand a text.

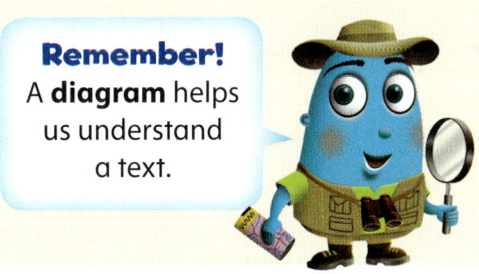

A Read. Look at the diagram.

My Autobiography

My name is Soo-Mi. I'm from Korea.
I like animals and games.

These are my parents.
This is my Aunt Yu-Na.
She's fun.

This is Jin-Joo. She's
my sister. She's tall.

This is my grandmother,
and he's my grandfather.
He's 95 years old!

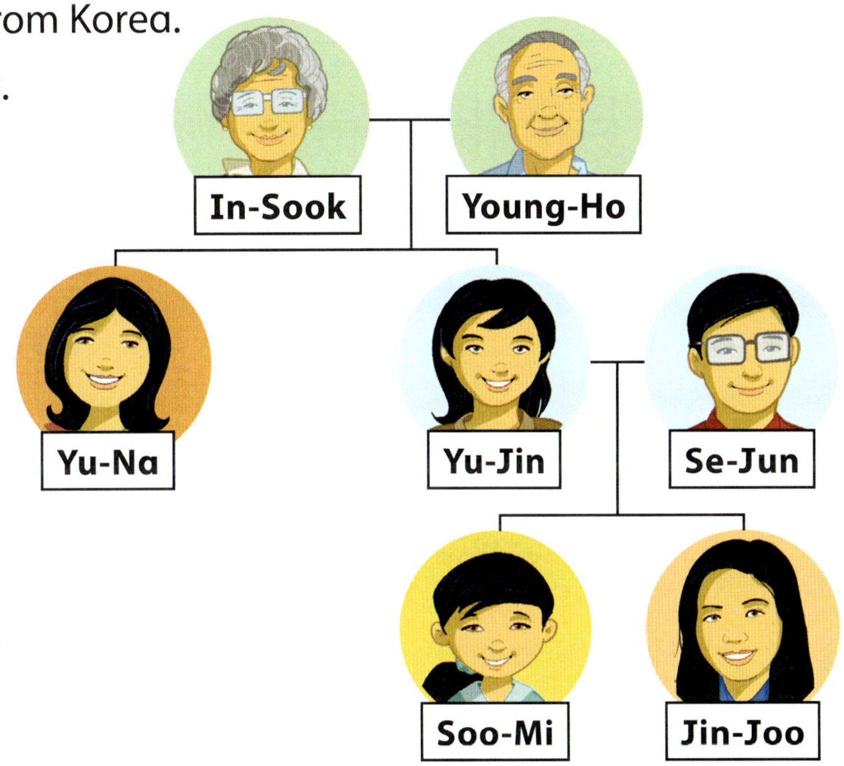

In-Sook
Young-Ho
Yu-Na
Yu-Jin
Se-Jun
Soo-Mi
Jin-Joo

B Read again. Then choose the correct answer.

1. Soo-Mi's aunt is fun.	(Yes)	No
2. Soo-Mi's sister is little.	Yes	No
3. In-Sook is Soo-Mi's grandmother.	Yes	No
4. Se-Jun is Jin-Joo's grandfather.	Yes	No
5. Soo-Mi has a brother.	Yes	No
6. The diagram shows Soo-Mi's family.	Yes	No

C Complete the sentences.

grandfather   aunt   grandmother   ~~sister~~

1.

    She's my _____sister._____

2.

    This is my _____

3.

    He's my _____

4.

    This is my _____

D Complete the sentences.

1. This is my _sister_____. She's funny.

2. He's my _g_____. He likes animals.

3. This is my _g_____. She's 80 years old.

4. She's my _a_____. She's my father's sister.

Write

Circle _I_ and _my_.

I'm eight years old.
This is my sister.

Remember!
Use _I_ and _my_ to write
about your life.

Picture Dictionary

Write the key words.

Unit 1

_____

_____

_____

_____

Unit 2

_____

_____

_____

_____

Unit 3

_____

_____

_____

_____

Unit 4

_____

_____

_____

_____

Picture Dictionary

Unit 5

_____
_____

_____
_____

_____
_____

_____
_____

Unit 6

_____
_____

_____
_____

_____
_____

_____
_____

Unit 7

_____
_____

_____
_____

_____
_____

_____
_____

Unit 8

_____
_____

_____
_____

_____
_____

_____
_____

Unit 9

_____
_____
_____

_____
_____
_____

_____
_____
_____

_____
_____
_____

Unit 10

_____
_____
_____

_____
_____
_____

_____
_____
_____

_____
_____
_____

Unit 11

_____
_____
_____

_____
_____
_____

_____
_____
_____

_____
_____
_____

Unit 12

_____
_____
_____

_____
_____
_____

_____
_____
_____

_____
_____
_____

Syllabus

Topic	Unit	Reading Goal	Key Words	Writing Goal
TOPIC 1 In Your School	Unit 1	Look at the pictures	*desk, bookcase, chair, wastebasket*	Write a short paragraph
	Unit 2	Find the numbers	*pencil case, pencil, crayon, marker*	Focus: Capital letters and periods
TOPIC 2 Animals	Unit 3	Read the title	*dog, cat, bird, hamster*	Write an informational paragraph
	Unit 4	Read the captions	*horse, frog, turtle, rabbit*	Focus: Pictures and captions
TOPIC 3 Colors and Shapes	Unit 5	Find the color words	*orange, black, purple, pink*	Write a description
	Unit 6	Find the shape words	*rectangle, oval, heart, triangle*	Focus: Descriptive words
TOPIC 4 What Do You Like?	Unit 7	Find the topic	*jump rope, doll, robot, yo-yo*	Write a friendly letter
	Unit 8	Find the details	*smoothie, juice, pizza, cake*	Focus: Commas
TOPIC 5 How's the Weather?	Unit 9	Find the differences	*cold, snowy, sunny, hot*	Write a weather report
	Unit 10	Find the cities	*rainy, cloudy, windy, storm*	Focus: Time words
TOPIC 6 Family and Friends	Unit 11	Find the characters	*father, mother, baby sister, brother*	Write an autobiography
	Unit 12	Use a diagram	*aunt, sister, grandmother, grandfather*	Focus: *I* and *my*